K. M. Weld

Lily the lost one

The fatal effects of deception

K. M. Weld

Lily the lost one
The fatal effects of deception

ISBN/EAN: 9783741188435

Manufactured in Europe, USA, Canada, Australia, Japa

Cover: Foto ©Andreas Hilbeck / pixelio.de

Manufactured and distributed by brebook publishing software (www.brebook.com)

K. M. Weld

Lily the lost one

LILY THE LOST ONE.

LONDON: BURNS AND OATES.

See Page 282.

THE LOST ONE

FATAL EFFECTS OF DECEPTION.

MARK WELD,

LILY THE LOST ONE;

OR,

THE FATAL EFFECTS OF DECEPTION.

BY

MISS K. M. WELD,
THE WRITER OF "BESSY."

LONDON: BURNS & OATES.
1881.

PREFACE.

—o—

THIS little Tale may be considered an illustration of the simple lines, so familiar to each one of us—

> "Oh! what a tangled web we weave,
> When first we practise to deceive."

CONTENTS.

---o---

CHAPTER	PAGE
I. AN UNEXPECTED GUEST	1
II. THE SUDDEN SHOCK	12
III. THE MYSTERY	24
IV. THE REBUFF	34
V. THE APPROACHING CLOUD	44
VI. RETURN OF ALICE	55
VII. TROUBLES WITH ALICE	77
VIII. ALICE'S IGNORANCE	89
IX. LILY LOSES HER ONLY FRIEND	106
X. FRESH SORROWS ARISE	115
XI. LIFE OF LILY AT THE FARMHOUSE	131
XII. THE MILLINER	161
XIII. SAD CATASTROPHE CAUSED BY JEALOUSY—TAKES REFUGE WITH AN OLD APPLE-WOMAN	188
XIV. A KIND FRIEND	210
XV. MISS SINCLAIR EDUCATES LILY	224
XVI. FRESH TRIALS AND ANXIETY	237
XVII. SCENE IN PORTLAND PLACE	263
XVIII. ST. ELIZABETH'S HOSPITAL	271

CHAPTER	PAGE
XIX. THE HISTORY OF THE STRANGER	295
XX. CONTINUATION OF THE HISTORY OF THE STRANGER	325
XXI. THE VOYAGE OUT	334
XXII. THE CAPTURE AND IMPRISONMENT	361
XXIII. THE RELEASE	374

LILY, THE LOST ONE;

OR,

THE FATAL EFFECTS OF DECEPTION.

CHAPTER I.

AN UNEXPECTED GUEST.

"CLOSE the shutters, double bar the hall door, shut every window carefully, and then we will go into the parlour and have a comfortable hot supper, Mrs. Heslope, for it is vain to look out for travellers of any description on such a fearfully stormy night. Listen to the wind, how it whistles round the corner of the house; thank God we are on dry land—not out at sea. God help the poor unfortunate sailors who may be exposed to such a tremendous gale! I fancy I hear thunder in the distance—it can be nothing else; no one in their senses would venture out on such a night."

These words were spoken by the fat, burly, good-humoured landlord of a small inn in a remote village in a mountainous part of North Wales, and addressed to his wife, whose exterior certainly formed a complete contrast to his own; for her spare figure, pinched-in nose, and screw mouth, seemed to indicate both a bad temper and a parsimonious disposition. The genêral opinion was, that the face of the lady did not belie her, and that if her husband had not been the very essence of good nature and general amiability, quarrels must have been of more than frequent occurrence; but, as it was, they pulled together pretty well; he seldom answered when she scolded, but waited quietly to the end, and then asked some question on a totally different subject, so as to divert her thoughts from the cause of anger. This plan often succeeded; the tremendous storm passed over, and the sky became by degrees serene and peaceful. Some persons considered him weak, and thought he yielded too easily, but others, on the contrary, who observed matters more closely, saw that although, for the sake of peace, he acceded to her wishes in minor points, yet that in any matter of real importance he would not be bullied into acting against his judgment or conscience; he let her talk and scold as much as she pleased, but insisted on his commands being carried out. In the commencement of their married life she called tears and even "high strikes" to her aid, but soon discovered that such manifestations of wrath did not forward her wishes, for the more she cried the louder he laughed; even fainting had no effect, save causing him to leave the room and pay his stables a visit, while he left her to recover at her leisure, and by degrees she gave up such displays of temper.

Mr. Heslope had kept the hotel about ten years, and was in a pretty good way of business, as his house was much frequented during the summer months by gentlemen who came to that part of the country for fishing. His wife was a good cook and an excellent manager; he was universally popular on account of his kind heart and great honesty; therefore if gentlemen once made his hotel their headquarters for a month or so, they were pretty certain to return the following year, and he preferred old customers.

However we must return to the evening in

question. Mrs. Heslope glanced disdainfully at her husband, and replied:

"Go into the parlour if you please, Mr. Heslope; make yourself as comfortable as you please, but I shall not shut up yet. My ears are sharper than yours; it is not thunder, it is not wind that you hear in the distance—it is the rumble of wheels, the tramp of horses, and occasionally the crack of a whip."

"Fudge, fudge, missus! Merely imagination! fudge, fudge! But 'the wilful woman must have her way,' as the old song says."

He left the kitchen and was going towards the parlour, when he stopped suddenly and listened attentively for a few moments.

"Sure enough, she's right for once!" he exclaimed, and hurried back to his wife. She was standing exactly where he left her, and when he said, "You are quite right, my dear, your ears are better than mine," she deigned not a reply, but continued to listen, for it was useless to look out, as the night was so dark that a person could scarcely see his own hand; the snow was falling in large flakes, and the boisterous wind rushed through the house if the door was opened even for a moment. By degrees the sounds became more and more distinct, and all doubt ceased when a carriage, drawn by two horses, drove up to the door, which was immediately opened by the landlord, who went out and opened the carriage door, inviting the occupants to descend.

There were two persons seated in this carriage, a lady and a child of apparently six or seven years of age. The lady was attired in deep mourning; she was young, apparently worn out with fatigue, but had a handsome aristocratic countenance. The little girl was fast asleep, nestled against her mother's bosom; she was fair as a lily, and you might easily imagine her to be a sleeping angel, so sweet and innocent was her appearance. The landlord put down the carriage steps and said:

"Will you be pleased to alight, madam?"

"Yes," she answered; "I wish to remain at your hotel for the night, and I shall continue my journey to-morrow morning."

She awoke the child, bade her get out of the carriage, and then descended herself with the assistance of the landlord's arm, for she seemed so weak as to be almost unable to stand. The landlord supported her frail figure and conducted her to his wife, who was standing within the door ready to greet the unhoped-for guests.

Mrs. Heslope was about to address the stranger, and bid her welcome with great volubility, when she perceived that she was almost fainting, and therefore desired Phœbe (the sole servant) to bring the arm-chair out of the parlour. She placed the lady carefully in it, offering her at the same time a little warm wine and water; but she merely tasted it.

Meantime the landlord bustled up, and begged to know whether he was to pay the post-boy for the hire of the carriage and horses, likewise whether she wished it to be ordered for the following day.

She looked at him in a bewildered manner as if scarcely understanding his words, but after a short pause replied—

"What is the charge? I will pay at once; I shall not require it to-morrow if you can furnish me with a carriage to proceed on my journey."

The landlord returned to the man, who said that the charge his master usually made for a carriage and pair for that distance was twelve shillings, but that in such weather he would not send out his horses under fifteen; and that he had told the lady so when she took his carriage.

"Likewise," added he, "surely no lady can refuse to give a trifle to boot to the poor chap who drove her through this storm."

The landlord told the lady what the man said; she opened her purse, took out a sovereign, put it into his hand, and replied—

"Give him this, and let him keep the change; it is indeed a fearful night."

The landlord started, offered to return the sovereign, and said quickly—

"But it is too much, my lady; the fellow will be quite satisfied with a couple of shillings."

The stranger raised her dark blue eyes and looked at him. He thought he had never before seen such a touching expression of countenance,—deep misery was coupled with the greatest sweetness; but she signed him to keep the coin, and arose and approached the fire, apparently to warm herself.

The landlord took the sovereign to the man, who eyed it with delight and exclaimed—

"She's a brick! that she be's. Won't I drink her health, and that of the young 'un too."

The landlord asked whether he would not put up his horses for the night, but he shook his head and drawled out—

"Na; I means to go on two miles farther. There I know an old lodger who'll take in I and my 'osses for little or nothing; so ge I quick a glass of summat warm, and I'll drink to your very good health and be off in no time at all."

The landlord looked compassionately at the poor, jaded, wretched horses, which seemed scarcely able to stand from fatigue and cold, and said—

"Surely you will give an hour's rest and some hay and water at least to those worn-out beasts; they can never go two miles farther with this cold north wind blowing through them?"

"Na, na, they be's used to it. I'll touch 'em up a bit when we're off, and they'll go it well enough."

The landlord saw it was useless to say more, therefore he gave the man the glass of spirits, which he swallowed quickly, and then jumped on the coach-box and commenced shouting loudly, accompanying each shout with a volley of slashes with his long whip on

the reeking sides of the unfortunate horses.
Maddened by fear and pain, they sprang
forward and were quickly out of sight; but,
the storm continuing with unabated force, they
slackened their pace, and as the darkness of
the night prevented the coachman from guiding them properly, the carriage was suddenly
plunged into a deep chasm by the side of the
road. No efforts were sufficient to extricate it,
and there they were obliged to remain; and
there we will leave them.

The gold so liberally given by the stranger
raised her immensely in the estimation of the
landlady, who immediately inquired, in the
most deferential manner, how many rooms were
required, and what refreshment she could offer
to herself and the young lady.

The stranger appeared so exhausted by the
fatigue of her journey as scarce to be able to
speak above a whisper; but she roused herself,
looked at the landlady for a moment, and said—

"Prepare one room with a good-sized bed;
my child will sleep with me."

"And what refreshments may I offer your
ladyship?"

"A basin of warm soup will be sufficient for

myself and my child. Let us have it quickly, for we are terribly fatigued with the journey. We shall then go to our room; therefore I wish to have it prepared as soon as possible. And let us have a good fire."

The landlady bustled off, summoned her maid-servant Phœbe, ordered the best room in the inn to be made ready, and then returned to the kitchen to prepare some savoury soup, which she carried with a plate of dry toast to the parlour. The lady swallowed a very small quantity, but was unable to take more; the child, however, drank it with smiling delight, and began immediately to talk and smile, made herself quite at home, and begged for a few cakes before finishing her repast. The landlady immediately brought forth her best on a little tray, and presented them to the child, who smiled and said, "Thank you; oh! what a pretty tray!"

The stranger arose, took the hand of her child, and said, "I will go upstairs at once; show me my room."

"At what hour do you wish to be called, and to have your hot water in the morning, my lady?" said the landlady obsequiously.

"Do not call me at all; let no one come near our room or disturb us with hot water, or anything else, until I ring the bell. I suppose there is a bell in the room?"

Unfortunately there was not such a thing, and the landlady was obliged to own the fact with many blushes and excuses.

"How inconvenient," said the stranger; "but at least you must have a hand-bell?"

"There is no bell in the house, my lady, but the dinner-bell, and that is cracked."

"Well, never mind, that will do better than nothing at all. You can put it on the table by the side of my bed, and Lily shall not ring it very loud."

The landlady fetched the huge, rusty, cracked bell, and little Lily clapped her tiny hands with delight when she heard the discordant sound that emanated from the ugly old-fashioned concern. It was put on the table on her side of the bed, and she laughed as she anticipated the fun she should have in ringing it in the morning.

CHAPTER II.

THE SUDDEN SHOCK.

THE sun shone brightly on the following morning, the wind was hushed, and the only indication of the late tempestuous night was the thick mantle of snow which covered the ground as far as you could see;—trees, hedges, houses were white and sparkling from the effects of the rays of the unclouded sun.

The landlady was up and about very early, walking to and fro, and making arrangements for what might be required for the breakfast of the lady and her child. "Let me see," she mentally ejaculated, "what shall I give 'em? I will not propose eggs and bacon, that would be too vulgar for such a fine lady—no; and she'd perhaps turn up her nose if I proposed the cold round of salt beef. What shall I prepare, Phœbe?"

"I should say, missus, that you had best roast a little pullet; it would look nice and delicate."

"The very thing, Phœbe; see about it at once,—lose no time. Pullets are dear at this time of the year, but what does that signify to a lady who pulls out a sovereign like a sixpence? But it is getting late,—it is almost eight o'clock. I do not hear a sound in the room. Well, no matter, she must not be disturbed on any account. Perhaps she will be too tired to continue her journey; but that will be all the better for my purse, say I."

Nine o'clock struck; still no sound was heard in the room in which the desolate-looking lady and her fair child were sleeping. Half-past nine! no sound still. The landlord had long finished his breakfast, and went to the stables to look to his horses. His wife fidgetted about from the kitchen to the parlour, then back to the kitchen, and finally went upstairs to find Phœbe, and consult her as to what was best to be done.

"That lady told me so decidedly not to enter her room in the morning until she rang the bell, that I do not like even to knock at the door for fear of disturbing her. What do you think, Phœbe—would you knock at the door?"

"No, mum, I shouldn't; I would wait a bit. The poor lady did look so dead tired last night; she trembled like a leaf as she walked upstairs. I longed to offer her my arm, but feared she might think me bold. Such a fine elegant creature, too! But oh! what a sad look in her face. I never can forget that look if I live a hundred years; her beautiful eyes filled with tears every now and then. The child looked a merry little 'grig' enough, but she clung to her mother, who held and seemed almost to fear losing her."

"Dear me, Phœbe, how you do chatter; when you once begin to talk you never know when to stop. The lady looked tired enough, no doubt, but as for beauty of any kind I remarked none; I never do. I care not two straws for beauty; I only hope she will order plenty while she is here, and pay her bill honestly when she goes; that is of more consequence than all the beauty in the world—'handsome is as handsome does,' as my poor mother used to say."

Phœbe turned round and continued dusting and sweeping the room, while the landlady went into the yard to call her husband and tell him that she was beginning to get quite uneasy at the silence in the room of the strange lady. He bade her have patience, and not call him in for such trifles; in truth, he was rather put out at having to leave his horses just as the hostler was measuring out their corn; he always saw each horse fed himself, as he knew by experience the tricks which grooms play with the horses and their food if not narrowly watched.

Ten o'clock at length struck; still no sound was heard. Phœbe looked at her mistress with evident alarm painted on her countenance, and this time the mistress felt so really frightened that she could not express her feelings. She despatched Phœbe to bid Mr. Heslope come upstairs without delay, to accompany her to endeavour to ascertain the cause of the long silence.

He came at once, and seeing that she was really uneasy, said—

"Well, my dear, I daresay all is right, the lady is only over-fatigued; but you and Phœbe must enter the room, and I will stand outside in case you require any assistance or she wishes me to fetch a doctor."

The mistress and Phœbe stood undecidedly at the door for a few moments, and then gave a gentle tap; but no answer was returned. They opened the door softly, and noiselessly entered the room. The bed was an old-fashioned four-posted one, with curtains all round, and these curtains were so closely drawn that the person in bed could not be seen when you first entered the room. Mrs. Heslope, with Phœbe behind her, walked up to the bed and drew aside a small portion of the bed-hangings, but both started and recoiled at the sight which met their gaze. The lady was lying stretched out as if in a sound sleep, but they saw at once that she was dead—quite dead. Her long dark hair fell loosely on the pillow and over the side of the bed, her mouth was half open, and her eyes fixed; she seemed to have died without a struggle, for there was not a symptom of convulsion in her face. One hand was outside the sheet, and held a smelling-bottle; she seemed to have passed away in the act of trying to relieve her probable feeling of faintness by inhaling the saltz.

The child was apparently but just awake; she looked fresh and blooming as a newly-expanded rose, and was looking at her mother in surprise, thinking her in a sound sleep, puzzled by the fixed eyes, but yet without the slightest comprehension of what the case really was. The curly flaxen hair of the child fell over her face and mingled with the glossy brown hair of the corpse as she leant over it. When the landlady and Phœbe came up to the bed, she held up her tiny finger and said in a whisper—

"Hush, hush! mammy sleep. Poor mammy, so tired! Hush! do not wake mammy."

Alas! poor child, she did not know the fearful sorrow that was come upon her; she did not know that her mother would never wake again, that never would she again receive a caress from that tender mother; that she was left alone, uncared for, an orphan in this dreary world, with no one to love, no one to watch over her, no one to teach, with gentle sweetness, the great truth that this world is but a place of passage to our true home—to that happy country where tears shall be no more, and where alone we shall find that peace, that unchanging happiness, which is so often sought, but never found, in this bleak and dreary world, into which this poor child was now thrown, like a bark without an anchor on the stormy ocean.

Tears coursed one another down the rough sunburnt cheeks of Phœbe as she looked at the innocent, unsuspecting child; even the landlady was touched, and said to Phœbe—

"I will go downstairs and send for the doctor, that he may see whether there is anything to be done for this poor lady; it is possible that it may be simply a fainting fit; perhaps she is not really dead, perhaps bleeding may restore consciousness; at all events, we can but try."

Phœbe shook her head mournfully; having seen death so often, she was certain there was not a shadow of hope, but returned no answer, being fully aware that any difference in opinion would not be allowed by her mistress.

"Phœbe," continued Mrs. Heslope, "during my absence you must endeavour to persuade the child to leave her mother, as she cannot be allowed to remain during the visit of the doctors, for whom I am now going to send. You will probably have difficulty in making her do this, but it must be done either by kind words or by force if necessary."

The landlady bustled out of the room and

Phœbe approached the poor child, who was beginning to look terribly frightened at the protracted sleep of her mother, and at her pale and ghastly appearance.

"It is time for you to get up and be dressed, my child," said Phœbe gently. "Come with me, and when you are dressed and have had your breakfast you shall come back to mamma."

"No, no," answered the poor child quickly, "Lily will not leave dear mammy, she will stay till mammy wakes, and be so quiet too. Lily does not want breakfast, she only loves dear mammy—darling mammy. Lily will kiss dear mammy gently, oh! so gently."

She bent her little head over her poor mother and imprinted a soft kiss, but the cheek was cold, deadly cold—the icy cold of death. The child started, turned pale, burst into tears, and exclaimed—

"Oh, mammy so cold! poor mammy, so cold!"

"Yes, dear child," said Phœbe, "mammy is very cold. Come with me and I will look for a warm blanket to wrap round her, and how nice and warm she will then be. Come along, dear."

The child hesitated, looked again at her mother, and said—

" Lily cannot leave mammy, no, no ! "

But at last Phœbe persuaded the reluctant child to leave the room to look for the warm blanket, and when they were safely upstairs, fetched some breakfast, which the child ate on being assured that it was necessary before starting again on her long journey.

"But Lily would like her breakfast in mammy's room, by mammy's bed."

" No, dear child," said Phœbe, "you might disturb mammy, she is so tired, and very ill too; the doctor has been, and he says she must be kept quite quiet—that no one must go into the room, not even you. You would not like to hurt mammy, I am sure, and she might die, and you do not wish mammy to die."

" To die! what do you mean by 'to die' ? "

" Have you never seen anything dead ? "

"Oh yes, I saw my white duck when it was dead ; but mammy is not a duck, so why should she die ? "

"We must hope not, my dear child ; but remember how cold poor mammy was when you kissed her. Sometimes when persons get cold like that, it is because they are ill, and if they get very, very ill, it is because God thinks it is time for them to go to Heaven. Perhaps God has told mammy to come to Him in Heaven."

"Oh no! I am certain mammy would not leave Lily."

"When God calls, dear child, we must leave everything; you know we must obey God."

"Oh yes, mammy always said we must love God with our whole heart, and do everything He tells us to do; but I am sure God will not take away my mammy, He is too good for that."

"God does all that is right, my child, and you love Him, and if He told you that mammy would be more happy in Heaven than on earth, you would let her go, I know."

"I am sure mammy would not be happy to leave Lily."

"But did not mammy say that God knew best about everything, and that we must go to Him directly He called? and if He has called mammy now, He will, perhaps, soon call you too."

"But God has not called mammy—has He?"

The child turned pale as she said this, and burst into tears.

"Oh, please say God has not called dear mammy to go to Him in Heaven."

"I cannot say so, dear child, for I fear He has; remember how cold she was when you kissed her. Persons are always cold like that when they are dead."

"O mammy, mammy!" shrieked the poor child; "please come back from Heaven and take Lily; do not leave Lily."

She sobbed convulsively, ran to the door and tried to get out, but it was locked; all her efforts were ineffectual, she could not turn the key. Phœbe did all in her power to soothe the poor child, who continued to exclaim, in a heart-rending voice—

"Take me to mammy; oh, take me to mammy in Heaven!"

She did not seem to doubt the death of her mother—to doubt her mother being called to Heaven—for the remembrance of the deathly cold of the pallid face when she kissed it was full in her mind. But she entreated Phœbe's permission to go, at least, and look once more at the mother she had left, as she then thought, sleeping, but Phœbe could not consent; she knew it was impossible to allow such a thing, as the doctors were arrived, and were examining the corpse to ascertain the cause of death, previous to the coroner's inquest; but she quieted the child by promising that if she would lie down on the bed and try to sleep for a little time, she should then return to look at her mother. The child consented, and sobbed herself by degrees into a dull, heavy sleep.

CHAPTER III.

THE MYSTERY.

THE two doctors who had been sent for arrived and were immediately conducted to the room where the corpse was lying; nothing had been moved, but the doctors ordered the shutters to be opened for the admission of more light, and then proceeded at once to examine the corpse, in order to ascertain the immediate cause of death.

After a long and careful examination, and having heard all the particulars of her arrival the night before, they pronounced that death was caused by disease of the heart, probably accelerated by grief and terror of some kind.

The coroner's inquest was then held over the body; and the verdict returned was, "Death by the visitation of God."

The landlady begged that arrangements might be made for having the funeral as soon as possible, on account of the inconvenience of having a corpse in her hotel.

A meeting of the local magistrates was called to decide what was to be done with the child, that they might examine her, and endeavour to obtain some clue as to what relations she had, and where she could be sent instead of going to the workhouse. The deep snow rendered the roads almost impassable, therefore the meeting was not held until late in the afternoon. Four magistrates were present at it; and after hearing all the particulars of the distressing case, they desired the landlord to bring the child into court, that they might endeavour, by questions, to ascertain where the lady came from, and whether there were any relations who would claim her child.

She was immediately brought into the hall by Phœbe. She looked flushed and frightened, and clung to the kind-hearted servant's arm; but she had ceased crying, and as the magistrates looked at her kindly, and spoke gently, she answered their questions readily and simply, almost as if she hoped that they might bring her mother back, and make her again happy.

The chief magistrate, a grey-headed, benevolent-looking old man, commenced his interrogations thus—

"What is your name, my little girl?"

"Lily."

"Yes, but what else?"

"Oh! nothing else."

"What was the name of your father and mother?"

"Only mamma and papa."

"But what did the servants call them?"

"Missus and master."

"Where did you live?"

"In a small house, such a pretty one, with a honeysuckle round the door, and a great hill behind, and a pond with lots of white ducks on it, and pappy gave me one duck for my own."

"Hush, child, we do not want to hear about your ducks."

"Oh, how funny, I thought every one loved ducks; but do please send me home, perhaps papa will be come back by this time."

"But cannot you remember the name of your home, and of your papa?"

"They sometimes called our house the Cottage, and mammy often called papa dear Willie, but generally darling, or love."

"How many servants had you?"

"Only cook and nurse. Nurse went away, and then mamma dressed me, and gave me my bread and milk."

"When did your papa leave you?"

"Oh, before nurse went away, and mammy did cry so, and Lily cried too, oh! so much;" and at these words the poor little child burst into tears, and exclaimed between her sobs, "Oh, do send me home, do please send me home, papa will come back some day, I know he will, mammy said he would."

"My dear child," replied the chief magistrate, "we would most willingly send you to your home, if you could tell us where it is, or the name of your father. Were there no houses near your cottage?"

"Oh yes; old lame Tom lived in a wee, wee house, with his blind mother, on the other side of the hill behind our cottage; and old Molly Smith lived near the bog—there was no one else."

"Well, this does not help us much, little girl; but why did your mother leave your home?"

"I do not know; mammy said to cook one

day: 'I must go at once; the letter I received this morning almost killed me with fear. I must hide somewhere until William returns—if he ever returns—but alas! I have not heard from him since Christmas.'"

"Well, my little girl, try and remember something more; what did cook say?"

"Cook said, 'You are right, madam; go quickly, but do not tell me where you intend to live; they might come here and question me,—write in a few months, and tell me where you are.' Then they began to whisper something, and I ran out of the house to look at my ducks, and I determined if mamma went away to take mine with me in a basket."

"Well, well, never mind, child, about the ducks, but tell me when did you and your mamma set off on your journey?"

"On a Friday,—I am sure it was Friday, for cook said, quite loud, 'Lausy me, mum, do not go on a Friday, it is sure to bring you bad luck;' but mammy only smiled, and said, 'How can you be so silly?'

"I had my supper at five that day instead of six; and directly I had finished we got into a carriage and drove off. But mammy would not let me take my duck after all; she said she would give me plenty more some day."

"Did you drive through any towns?"

"What is a town, sir?"

"A great many houses together."

"It was quite dark when we first set off, but in the morning when it was light, mammy always pulled down the blinds when she saw any houses coming. I was sorry, for I wished to look at them, the day was so long; but we went on, on, on. At last it got dark again, and then I went to sleep; and then the next morning it was snowing hard, and I was so cold, and I cried, but that did no good. We stopped twice that day, and a man brought some cakes to the carriage-door. Then it began to get dark and colder and colder, and the snow fell fast. I begged mammy to go home again, but she said, 'No, no, child, be quiet, child;' so I sat quietly and went to sleep again long before we arrived at this place."

"But when you were at home, before your papa went away quite, did he always stay with you and your mamma?"

"Oh, dear, no! He often went away for a long time, and we were always so glad when he came back; and he was sure to bring such pretty presents for mammy and me. Oh! do send me home, I daresay I shall find him returned by this time."

"It is a strange thing," said the elder of the magistrates, turning to the three other gentlemen; "it is evident that for some mysterious reason this child has been kept in total ignorance of her father's and mother's name, and of the place where they lived. It must be so, for the child is of an age to know such things unless purposely concealed from her; and she seems intelligent, although innocent and simple as a child would be if brought up quite in the country, with no associates but birds and flowers. It is a strange, a very strange case; but I see nothing that we can do in the matter. You know, of course, that the verdict given by the coroner with regard to the mother was that she died by the visitation of God. Her small travelling-box has been opened and examined. It contained only a few articles of dress, all of the finest material, but afforded no clue for the discovery of anything,—there were no papers of any kind, only ten pounds in her purse, and she wore a few trinkets besides her wedding ring. Round the neck of the child was a very small miniature of a gentleman, which she says is her papa. That, however, tells nothing; it is a good painting, but there is no writing inside,—not the slightest clue to what he was or to what he is. The landlord has endeavoured to trace the carriage, but in vain; no one saw it after it left his inn. It is possible that during that dark night they may all have fallen over into one of the deep chasms in the mountain sides, and if so they of course perished miserably. I see nothing more that we can do in the matter. The lady must be buried and the child go to the workhouse; there is no help for it."

The other magistrates did not reply, but looked with compassion at the poor motherless child; each wished he could do something for her, but no one did more than mutter, "Poor child, poor child." They were mostly gentlemen of small means, and with families of their own, who could not think of encumbering themselves with a penniless strange child.

The silence remained unbroken, when the landlord stood up and asked leave to speak. It was quickly granted, and he said—

"Gentlemen, I am but a poor man, as you know. My inn is in rather an unfrequented locality, therefore my visitors are few and my gains small; but I cannot turn this child whom Providence seems to have put into my hands adrift; my heart will not let me send her to the workhouse. I must trust in God, and hope that times may some day become better for me, but this child shall, for the present at least, have the shelter of my roof and a corner by my fireside. I will do by her as I do by my own child, come what may."

The gentlemen looked surprised at these words, and felt inwardly ashamed at being so completely outdone in generosity by the good landlord. His example moved them to do something in aid of the orphan,—they made a collection, and £10 were placed in his hands.

He thanked them for this assistance, and said, "Rest assured, gentlemen, that every penny shall be applied to her use. She may, and I hope will some day be discovered by her friends, but until that day comes I take charge of the poor innocent child. Come along, my dear, come with me."

Little Lily followed him instantly, and very gladly too, for the numerous interrogations had both puzzled and frightened her. They left the Court together and returned to the inn.

CHAPTER IV.

THE REBUFF.

THE kind heart of the good landlord, Mr. Heslope, had moved him to undertake the charge of the poor destitute child, but he had some misgivings in his own mind as to what his wife might think of the matter. He was not, however, left long in doubt, for she was at the door looking out for their return, and eyed little Lily in a most unpropitious manner.

"Well, what has been done about this child?"

"There was nothing to be done, my dear; every circumstance was examined into, but who the lady was remains a mystery."

"Well, of course they must bury her, and there's an end of that matter; but what will they do with the brat?"

"Nothing, my dear; I shall keep the poor child, and I hope you will be kind to her."

The Rebuff. 35

Mrs. Heslope was so completely astounded at these words, that she was unable even to reply for a few moments; but when at last she did recover her power of speech, she made good use of it.

"You old dolt, you old fool," she exclaimed, "what can you mean? Answer me quickly."

"I intend to keep the child, and bring her up as my own," answered the landlord quietly.

"Keep her! bring her up as your own! impossible! poor as we are; you must be dreaming, Mr. Heslope."

"Never was more wide awake in my life; therefore say no more, my dear, but give us a bit of dinner as quickly as you can. I am quite sure you would not really wish to send this poor child to the workhouse, you have too good a heart."

"None of your flummery for me, Mr. Heslope; I will have nothing to do with this beggar brat; I would send her to the workhouse at once—the right place for her."

"Listen to me, Mrs. Heslope, and these are my last words. If I refused the shelter of my roof to the poor, friendless innocent, whom God seems to have placed in my hands, I could not expect any blessing on my own child; and when I am called out of this life, to appear before the judgment seat of God, how could I expect Him to allow me to enter Heaven, as none but the merciful shall receive mercy; therefore say no more on the subject; but put this child in my daughter's bedroom until she returns, then we must see what other arrangement can be made."

Mr. Heslope said these words in that decided tone of voice which always made his wife feel that it was useless to endeavour to change his determination. On minor points she would dispute for hours, and generally gained the victory in the end; but she knew by experience that if her husband had made up his mind that a thing was his duty, neither tears, upbraidings, or anything else made any impression, so she turned her back contemptuously both on him and on poor little Lily, and returned to the kitchen to vent her ill-humour on Phœbe, or anything that came in her way. Both the cat and the dog had learned by experience to keep their distance, when the countenance of the mistress portended a storm, so the dog tucked its tail between its legs, and shrunk into its

The Rebuff. 37

kennel, and puss went into the yard to try and catch one of the numerous sparrows which were sitting twittering on some old barrels near the kitchen door, in hopes of a few crumbs being scattered among them, as the deep snow prevented the possibility of finding the food on which they usually subsisted.

Phœbe was obliged to remain, much against her own inclination, for everything she did was wrong in the eyes of Mrs. Heslope. She had boiled the potatoes when they ought to have been roasted, and roasted the joint which ought to have been boiled, the sauce was too thick, and the pie crust too thin. In vain did poor Phœbe plead that she had followed the orders of her mistress exactly, she was told to hold her tongue, that she was a deaf and stupid idiot.

A servant of the present day would have given her mistress notice at once, but Phœbe was a servant of that old school, who never gave up their situations for small grievances; besides which she was a good and religious woman, and knew that in this world all must expect a share of the cross; therefore she looked upon the temper of her mistress as that portion of the cross that our Lord called upon her to carry : so she tried to accept it cheerfully, and although depressed and worried at times soon recovered her usual equanimity of temper, and remained in the service of Mrs. Heslope. Fortunate it was for little Lily that she had done so, as no endeavours were wanting on her part to render the life of the poor child more comfortable, for although Mr. Heslope could insist on her remaining in his house, yet he could not prevail on Mrs. Heslope to show the child any kindness. She considered her an encumbrance, and grudged every penny that her husband spent upon her : she made the poor child work far too hard for one of her tender years, more especially one who had evidently been brought up in the enjoyment of every comfort. She would make her clean and scrub all the morning, and then in the afternoon, instead of allowing her a little walk to breathe the fresh air, or to take some slight recreation, she would shut her up alone in the back kitchen to do needlework.

Phœbe pitied the poor child extremely, and longed to help her in the various tasks imposed, but she did not venture to do much, for fear of exciting the anger of her mistress, and thus causing little Lily more suffering.

Often, however, when the poor child showed her the long task of needlework that had to be completed before the end of the week, she would rise an hour earlier in the morning, and stitch diligently in her own room, that Lily might not be obliged to work so hard to finish it.

But Phœbe did more than this, for being herself very well instructed on religious matters, she imparted all she knew to Lily. In her quiet simple way, she taught her everything necessary; and, above all, encouraged the poor child to confidence in God and conformity to His Divine will. Her words fell on a good soil and produced abundant fruit. The early impressions Lily had received from the example of her mother (which Phœbe soon discovered from the artless words and remarks of the child) had taken deep root, and the trials she now suffered seemed to strengthen them and bring them to maturity in her young mind.

However, the happiest time of the day was the evening, for then the kind landlord had usually a little leisure time, and he employed that time in teaching Lily many useful things. She could read and write a little when she first came, but he improved her very much, and taught her history, geography, and arithmetic besides. She made rapid progress, because he taught her kindly, and she was naturally quick and loved to learn. He seldom praised her in the presence of Mrs. Heslope, as he felt that any praise from him would arouse angry feelings, and render the position of the poor child more uncomfortable ; but he was not aware of half the hardships to which little Lily was subjected, as she never complained. He saw that she had not the light heart and cheerful spirits of other girls of her age, but that he attributed to the shock of the sudden death of her mother and the abandonment of her father. In his own mind he resolved to send her to some good school when he could afford it, but that was impossible at present; he had his own daughter to educate, and he could not do more for a stranger than for his own child ; so he resolved to leave things quietly as they were for the present. He often spoke to her of his daughter Alice, who was absent on a visit to an aunt who lived at a distance ; he said he hoped they would become great friends when she returned, and that he would teach them together.

Lily anticipated this with the greatest delight, and thought how pleasant it would be to have a companion for everything. She hoped that Alice would do a portion of the household work, and as it would be finished sooner, they could then walk out together and amuse themselves in the fresh air, and run and play, and gather wild flowers, as she remembered doing in former days when she lived so happily with her mother.

One evening Mr. Heslope told Lily that he hoped Alice would return home in the course of a few months. Lily was delighted, and ran to tell Phœbe, thinking she would rejoice with her, but Phœbe looked very grave, and said—

"Are you sure that Alice is really to return home soon?"

"Quite sure; but why do you look so grave? I thought you would be as pleased as I am. I felt sure that you would be delighted at my having a companion, for you know how sad I am sometimes when I have to sit and work all alone in that dark back kitchen. Of course, Alice will sit with me?"

Phœbe shook her head and made no answer. It was evident that she did not anticipate the return of Alice with pleasure, but she was silent, and told Lily she hoped that if Alice did return they would be happy together.

"But do tell me, Phœbe, why you look so grave and almost sad?"

"I do not wish you to look forward to Alice's return with too much pleasure, lest you should be disappointed; remember Alice is the daughter of Mrs. Heslope, and you are not. Alice will be allowed to do everything she pleases, and no one will contradict her; when she left home, she would obey no one, not even her father. If she chance to like you, she may make you much more happy; but if, as it is not impossible, she takes a dislike to you, she will have it in her power to make you very miserable."

"Oh, dear Phœbe! I will try to make her love me; I will do everything I can to please her; she must love me, I am sure she will."

"I hope so, my child; but you say you do all you can to please Mrs. Heslope, and do you think she loves you?"

"Oh no, no indeed, I am sure she does not," answered poor little Lily, bursting into tears; "but no little girl can be like Mrs. Heslope, who has rheumatism, which makes every one cross; a little girl must love to run and skip, and laugh and sing as I used when I lived with darling mamma. Now Alice will be with her mother, and that ought to make her happy and gay, although Mrs. Heslope is not nice, and beautiful, and kind, as my darling mamma was. Oh, why did God take her away from me, and leave me here all alone, where dear papa will never, I fear, find me?"

She took the little picture of her father, which Phœbe had fastened in a little pocket in the bosom of her stays, and kissed it over and over and over again, sobbing, and exclaiming—

"Oh, do, please God, tell father where I am, that he may come and fetch me, and take me to our home, and love me, and talk to me about dear mother, and that I may tell him all that has happened."

Phœbe pitied the distress of the poor child; she tried to comfort her, but it was evident that she had strong reasons for dreading the return of Alice, although she would say no more on the subject, which she knew must give pain.

CHAPTER V.

THE APPROACHING CLOUD.

A FEW sad years passed by, and Lily heard nothing more concerning the return of Alice, when one morning at breakfast Mrs. Heslope told her husband that she had received a letter from her sister, to say that Alice would return home on the following day.

"And what does your sister say about Alice?" was the answer; "does she say she is improved, that she is less headstrong and disobedient than formerly."

"Well, she does complain a little about her, but I do not think much of what my sister says; she is an old maid, and therefore, of course, very fidgety. There is not much amiss in Alice, for it is useless to attempt to put old heads on young shoulders."

"Your sister is a very sensible woman, my dear; she is no fidget, although she is an old maid; but Alice had very great faults when she left us,—she was not only heedless and idle, but also proud and jealous to a great degree. Much as I have always loved her, I deplore her tendency to these faults."

"Well, I declare, Mr. Heslope," said the mother angrily, "you are too bad, always complaining of my poor child. I believe you quite hate her, and it is to annoy me that you go on grumbling about her; she is quite as good as other girls of her age, as far as I can see. It's a pity you're not the father of that stupid wench Lily, whom you are always praising up to the skies, but whom I detest. I have hated that girl from the first moment I set eyes upon her; and I only wish some one would turn up and own her and rid us of such a nuisance."

"She is a good and inoffensive little girl; I cannot imagine why you dislike her. It must be from a spirit of contradiction."

Mrs. Heslope burst into angry tears, and declared she was the most ill-treated woman in the world,—that her husband hated both her and her child.

Mr. Heslope seeing that it was useless to say more on the subject rose and left the room, and Mrs. Heslope went to the kitchen to vent her ill-humour on little Lily, who was dusting the crockery as she had ordered her. She burst into the kitchen, and her sudden entrance startled the poor girl to such a degree, at the moment she was putting a tray of glasses on to a high shelf, that the start caused her to knock it against the side of the shelf, and two or three of the best tumblers fell on to the kitchen floor, and were of course broken into a thousand fragments. Mrs. Heslope did not take into consideration that her sudden and abrupt entrance had been the sole cause of the disaster, but she began to scold violently, and frightened Lily so much that in her haste to put the rest of the glasses safely on the shelf, she pushed the tray against the side of the wall, and down came all the rest of the glasses.

Mrs. Heslope seized Lily by the shoulders, and after boxing her ears until the poor girl could hardly stand, she pushed her into the back kitchen, locked the door, and determined she should remain there for the rest of the day and have no dinner. Mr. Heslope, who was in the yard, heard the clatter of the broken glass, and came in hurriedly to ask what had happened.

He arrived just after Mrs. Heslope had pushed Lily into the back kitchen, and asked in an angry tone, "Who had broken all that beautiful and expensive glass?"

Mrs. Heslope answered quickly—

"It was all broken by that young 'hussy' whom you are so fond of."

"But how did it happen, my dear?"

"It happened through her carelessness and disobedience, of course, Mr. Heslope. I have told her scores of times not to crowd the tray with too many glasses, when she is about to put them on the shelf; but she will always do it to save herself a little trouble. She was putting up the glasses with her tray much too full when I entered the kitchen,—down all the glasses slipped, as I had warned her they would; and now a pretty sum you will have to pay for this feat of your favourite."

Mrs. Heslope took care not to say that she herself had caused the accident by entering the kitchen suddenly and startling Lily. She was delighted to see how really angry her husband was, and continued—

"Such carelessness and disobedience must be punished, therefore I have locked her up in the back kitchen, and there she shall remain all day."

Mr. Heslope thought in his own mind that there were probably some extenuating circumstances, as Lily was usually so gentle and obedient, but he remained silent, afraid of incensing his amiable spouse still more, and decided in his own mind that a little punishment could do no harm, and might make her more careful in future. He did not know that Mrs. Heslope had struck her and intended to keep her without food all day.

Mrs. Heslope did not relent; in fact, she was pleased at being able to punish the child without interference on the part of her husband. She kept the kitchen door locked, and only entered it once to give her a long task of work to get through during the afternoon. At first the poor child could do nothing but sob and cry; by degrees she became more calm, and resolved to try and finish the long task she had to get through before bedtime.

She worked for some hours, but her head ached fearfully, and she began to get very hungry, for she had tasted nothing since her scanty breakfast at eight o'clock. She hoped

Mrs. Heslope would at least bring her a slice of bread; but no—hour after hour passed and no one entered the kitchen; it was almost seven o'clock, and she still sat there. A feeling of sickness and faintness came over her; she endeavoured to call some one, but no one was near to hear the weak trembling little voice which implored help. The faintness increased, she thought she was dying,—going to her mother, and a gleam of hope and happiness passed through her mind; it lasted but a moment, then all consciousness ceased, and little Lily fell on to the ground by the side of the stool on which she had been seated, and her work and materials were scattered around her.

Nine o'clock struck, and Mr. Heslope went out of the house to his stables. He asked no questions about Lily, he concluded she was in bed, and had had her supper long before. When he left the house, Mrs. Heslope thought she would go into the kitchen and send Lily up to bed, after giving her a few dry crusts to eat. The kitchen was so dark that scarcely anything could be seen by the light of the small lanthorn, but she concluded when she called Lily and received no answer, that the girl was asleep.

She approached closer, and seeing her on the floor concluded she had fallen down when asleep. She first gave the child a push with her foot, then called her sharply by name, and finally tried the effect of a shake, but all was vain, Lily neither answered nor moved. Mrs Heslope became really frightened when she saw the deathly pale face of the insensible form before her; she called Phœbe, who came quickly, and was seized with the deepest compassion at the condition of the poor child.

"Do you think she is dead, Phœbe?" said Mrs. Heslope in an agitated tone.

"I hope not," answered Phœbe quickly; "what has happened to the poor child? has she been ill this afternoon? I noticed she had not been upstairs once. I thought perhaps you were very busy and had kept her with you. But what have you done to her, mum, her face is so bruised?"

"Oh! I only gave her a little punishment as she broke some glasses, and I then shut her up here to work, but I hope she is not really dead! Perhaps she is only hungry, as Mr. Heslope and I thought it best she should be punished for her carelessness by having no dinner. I just brought her bread for supper."

"Upon my word, mum, I do think you have killed the child; I fear she will never revive, her hands are so deathly cold."

"O Phœbe! O Phœbe! do not alarm me so, what shall I do? What will my husband say, he will be so awfully angry,—and if she dies, they will take me before the court, and make out that I killed her, perhaps; but it's not my fault, I am sure, if she does die. Children must be punished if they break everything; but do stop chattering, Phœbe, and see what you can do for her."

"Let me have some hot brandy and water, mum. I will try to pour a little down her throat, it may have a good effect, and she must then be taken up to bed."

"Yes, yes, carry her up quickly before my husband comes in, and I will bring the brandy and hot water as soon as possible."

Phœbe took the poor child in her arms, went up stairs, and placed her tenderly on the bed. A little start soon showed that she was not dead, and a slight colour returned to the pale cheeks. Mrs. Heslope soon arrived with the hot brandy and water, for she was really frightened, and therefore willing for Phœbe to take any measures she thought advisable for the recovery of the poor child.

A little of the hot liquid was poured into a spoon, and put into Lily's mouth. As the fainting was caused by exhaustion, it soon revived her; she opened her eyes and looked round. At first she did not seem to recognise any one, or to know where she was, but said over and over again in an incoherent manner—

"Where am I, oh! where am I? Come down from heaven and fetch me, mammy, oh! do come, please, for I am ill, and so *very, very* unhappy."

Mrs. Heslope heard these words, and her conscience smote her; but she tried to silence it, and said to Phœbe—

"Give the child what you think best, and do not leave her until she is all right again. I shall go down stairs. No doubt the girl has been unhappy, but that was not my fault; it was because her father deserted her, of course,—as for punishing, of course she must be punished like other children when she does wrong."

Phœbe looked at her mistress sorrowfully and said, "She is not like other children, she has been brought up tenderly, and cannot bear rough treatment; if treated harshly she will certainly die."

"A beggar brat cannot expect to be pampered and treated like a lady. If she stays here she must work and rough it too. I only wish my dolt of a husband would send her off to the 'Union' at once; if she died there, no one would care a scrap, in fact they would rejoice at having one beggar less to keep."

Mrs. Heslope spoke more boldly now. She saw that Lily was recovering fast, and marched out of the room, banging the door so hard that it made the poor patient little sufferer start and burst into tears, but the tears relieved her, and she soon began to speak coherently, and asked Phœbe what had happened. By degrees the different events of the day flashed on her mind and she exclaimed, sobbing—

"Oh! why did not mother take me to Heaven, I begged her so—why did she not ask God to call me too?"

"Because, my dear, God wishes you to remain on earth a few years more. Perhaps before very long your father may discover where you are, and come to fetch you home, and then how happy you will be, and how he will rejoice; think of that, and do not wish to die before you see him again."

"Oh no, I should not like papa to come and find me dead too, but I cannot help wishing to go to dear mother, when I am very unhappy."

"Be patient, my child, try and bear all cheerfully, and God will, I feel sure, one day grant your prayer,—you will see your father again. Yes, I feel certain that some day you will once more be under the protection of that good father whom you loved so much, but be sure to take great care of the little picture you have of him, let no one see it,—it may be most valuable to you some day."

CHAPTER VI.

RETURN OF ALICE.

POOR little Lily passed an almost sleepless night, from the effects of her sufferings in the day, but towards morning she fell into a sound sleep, and was not roused as usual by the sharp voice of Mrs. Heslope calling her at six o'clock to get up and dress. No, her harsh mistress had been a little alarmed, and therefore thought she would let her remain in bed rather longer than usual, besides which she remembered different marks and bruises on the face of the child, caused partly by the blows she had given her and partly by the fall from her seat when she fainted, and Mrs. Heslope thought that if her husband saw these marks he would insist on knowing what had caused them; and she was very certain that little Lily, if questioned, would tell the exact truth, and then her stupid husband (as she termed him) would blame her and take the child's part.

Mr. Heslope had not been seated long at the breakfast table before he inquired why little Lily did not come down as usual.

"Well, the child seemed to me to have something of a cold this morning," answered Mrs. Heslope, "therefore I told her to remain in bed, and have her breakfast there."

Mr. Heslope opened his eyes rather in astonishment at such unusual kindness in his spouse, but thought it best to make no remark, and continued his breakfast. Suddenly, however, he turned to his wife, and said—

"Oh, by the by, how shall you manage to arrange a room for Lily, now that Alice is returning? The room she has is far too small for two."

"Of course it is, Mr. Heslope, and besides, you do not suppose I would allow that girl to sleep in the room with my daughter!"

"But how can we manage, my dear?"

"We must make up a bed in that room in the loft, which used to be the pigeon-house in your father's time."

"But that is such a miserable little hole, so

cold; and she would feel quite lonely. Cannot you arrange any other place, my dear, for her?"

"No; we want all the other rooms for travellers. I consider it quite good enough for her, and as for being lonely, you know very well that Phœbe is quite near."

"At all events, Mrs. Heslope, you must put a bit of carpet on the floor, as I know the boards are full of holes, and the wind blows through them terribly in the winter."

"I have no carpet to spare, Mr. Heslope, she must do without one."

But on this point Mr. Heslope was determined. He went himself to one of the bedrooms and took a square of carpet, which he carried up to the miserable little hole which was henceforth to be the bedroom of poor Lily, and he insisted on her bed being made comfortable, and with a sufficiency of bedding.

Mrs. Heslope was furious at what she termed his fidgetiness, and determined to go and tell Lily at once that she was to be turned out of her present bedroom. She therefore went there, banged open the door, and said—

"This is the last morning you will be in this

room, so bundle up your things as quickly as you can, and be off. My daughter Alice returns home to-day, this is her room, and it must be arranged for her occupation."

"But where am I to put my clothes, madam? where am I to sleep?" answered poor Lily, in a frightened tone of voice.

"You are to sleep in the little room in the loft, and you may think yourself well off that you have any room at all to sleep in. The workhouse is where you ought to be; the best place for you, too."

Lily felt sadly grieved at the thought of leaving her nice comfortable apartment; she had seen the room in the loft, too, and knew what a miserable little hole it was, in fact, it could hardly be called a room, as the rafters were bare, and there was only a species of window which had been put to block up the holes through which the pigeons used formerly to come in and out. The walls were not papered, merely whitewashed, and there were, as Mr. Heslope said, many holes in the floor through which the wind penetrated. The bit of carpet made it look rather more comfortable, but yet it was a dreary bedroom.

A hamper turned topsy-turvy stood in the middle of the room, and on this she was to put her jug and basin. There was one chair with a broken leg, and an old deal box, which Mrs. Heslope said would do quite well to hold her clothes, as there was no chest of drawers to spare. Her only comfort was the remembrance that Phœbe's room was very near, and that if she was either frightened or ill she could go to her. The sole treasures she possessed in the way of books consisted of two, her prayer-book and a book of simple tales given by her dear mother.

The poor child made no reply to the unfeeling words of her mistress, but proceeded to carry her scanty stock of clothing up to her new room without delay. The task was soon accomplished, and she then shut the door, sat down on the half-broken chair, and cried bitterly, —she cried because she felt so lonely, so wretched, so deserted; but she had not been in the room long before the door was softly opened, and Phœbe walked in, took the hand of the desolate child, and said—

"Cheer up, little Lily, do not grieve; you may make yourself quite happy here. Think of the stable where our Lord was born, that was far more bare and miserable than this room, and yet He who came down from Heaven was content with it, for our sakes; therefore you must accept this change willingly, because it makes you like Him,—and you must accept it cheerfully because our Lord loves those who are cheerful and good-humoured under every trial, whether great or small, which He thinks fit to send them; so, jump up, my dear, wipe away your tears, we will see if we cannot make the room look pretty comfortable. First, I will get Bill Slade to mend this chair, that you may sit on it without danger, then we will put this picture at the head of your bed."

As Phœbe said these words, she took from under her apron a rough print of our Lord on the cross, and His blessed Mother standing at the foot. Although the print was rather coarse, yet it had been taken from a good painting, therefore the expression both of the countenance of our Lord and that of His Mother was most devotional.

Little Lily thought it quite beautiful, and jumped up in an ecstacy of delight to thank Phœbe for bringing it.

"I am glad you like it," said the kind-hearted servant, "but what I wish you to do is this, whenever you meet with little troubles and disagreeables, do not lose your time in crying over them, but just look at our Lord on the cross, and say, 'Oh, my Saviour, I accept this from Thy hands,' and you will see how much more happy you will feel. I always do this when I am in trouble, and our Lord helps me. When Mrs. Heslope threw the mug of beer over me the other day, because (her husband having called me to do something else) I did not bring it as quickly as she expected, I felt very angry, and was on the point of telling her that I would not remain in her house another day, but the thought of our Lord, who said not a word when struck on the face, came suddenly into my mind, and instead of telling my mistress I would leave her at once, I ran upstairs and said a short prayer to beg our Lord to forgive and not to punish her ill-temper. You have no idea how happy I felt afterwards."

"Oh, dear Phœbe, I never can be as good as that; I will, however, try my best."

"Do so, my dear, and God will help you, but I hear a bustle below. I fancy Alice must be arrived; she will not find her father at home, he was obliged to go to a place at some distance to purchase flour."

"What shall I do, Phœbe? shall I go downstairs to see her? I hope she will speak kindly to me."

"I think it will be best for you only to go into the room to fetch the spoons that you were told to wash, perhaps Mrs. Heslope may then call you to speak to her daughter; but if she does not call you, I advise you to say nothing, but merely to take the spoons, wash them, and then put them back."

Lily obeyed, and went into the parlour with a beating heart. Alice was seated by the side of her mother, and they were talking and laughing together. Alice was apparently about fourteen years of age, rather short, very thick in figure, and with a red face and small turned-up nose; her appearance was decidedly not aristocratic; notwithstanding a very showy dress, a hat trimmed with a profusion of flowers, and a jacket of good material, she looked vulgar, decidedly vulgar.

"What do you want?" said Mrs. Heslope sharply, when Lily entered the room.

"If you please, I came for the spoons you told me to wash."

"Well, they are all in the cupboard, so take them out, and be off as quick as you can."

Lily advanced, opened the cupboard, and began to collect the spoons.

"Is that the girl you told me father was so stupid as not to let the magistrates send to the workhouse?"

"Yes, that's the girl."

"Law, what a pale, wretched creature," said Alice, looking with complacency at her own coarse, fat face in the glass.

"What's her name?"

"She said her name was Lily, and your father would have her called so; he fancied it might be the means of finding her father. I wished to call her Betty, it is a much better name for a servant—a mere beggar girl—but he wouldn't even hear of it; you know how obstinate father is when he once takes a fancy into his head."

"Yes, I know well enough, mother, but he shan't have his way this time. Lily is a young lady's name, so I will not call her Lily, that I'm determined; I shall call her Betty Union, that's where she ought to be, and Betty's just the name to fit her."

"Yes," answered Mrs. Heslope, "you are quite right, a girl like her ought to be called Betty or Bet, but you must not let your father hear you call her Betty, it would make him precious cross, I can tell you; he is so easily taken in, that he fancies the mother of this stupid girl was really a lady, and that her father will turn up some day and prove to be a grand lord, or duke, or something of the kind, but that's all nonsense. I do not believe her mother was a lady at all. At all events, if she really was, and was married to a gentleman, he must have deserted her, which comes to the same thing as having no husband at all, in my opinion; and, of course, if he left his wife, he must be glad enough to get rid of the child. He'll never turn up, worse luck!"

This conversation was carried on in a low tone whilst Lily was in the room, and she heard sufficient to cut her to the very heart, although she said nothing, but was carrying the spoons quietly out of the room to wash, when Alice bawled out in a mocking tone—

"I say, Betty Union, how are you off for soap?"

Lily had never before heard this vulgar, slang expression, therefore she was quite taken aback, but she returned to the door and said innocently, supposing that Alice wished to wash her hands after the long journey—

"Did you say, if you please, that you wished for some soap? there is none downstairs, but there is a piece in your bedroom. Shall I fetch it for you, with a basin and a towel?"

The boisterous laugh with which these words were received by both mother and daughter, made poor Lily quite confused, and not know what to answer, but she went out of the room again, and hastened upstairs to Phœbe, who was waiting for her.

"Well, my dear, have you seen Alice? and how do you like her?"

"O Phœbe! dear Phœbe! I have seen Alice, but she did not say one kind word; she only made game of me, and said I ought to be in the Union—I only wish I was, I am sure I should be more happy—and Mrs. Heslope said such cruel things, too, about my dear papa and mamma, and then, when I was going out of the room, Alice bawled out, 'Betty Union, how are you off for soap?' I thought she wanted a bit to wash her hands, but she did not, for when I offered to fetch some, they shouted, and laughed, and jeered so, that I ran out of the room, and I heard them laughing the whole way I went upstairs."

"I am very sorry," said Phœbe, "that Alice was not more kind, but I daresay she is in spirits at coming home again, and wanted a little fun. 'How are you off for soap?' is a vulgar, slang expression used by schoolboys. I daresay she heard it in the town where her aunt lives—it really means nothing at all—and she does not know how vulgar the expression is. I wonder her mother allows her to make use of it."

"Oh! but Mrs. Heslope laughed quite as loud as Alice."

"Well, think no more about it now; wash your spoons, and do not mind trifles."

"But do you think she will call me Betty Union? She said she would, and I should not like that at all."

"Perhaps she will, my dear, and if she does, I advise you to take it good-humouredly; for if she sees it makes you angry, she will persist in saying it the more, you may be sure of that; she will think it good fun."

"But that would be so ill-natured, Phœbe."

"She may not do it with an ill-natured intention, but, anyhow, take my advice and do not be cross if she calls you Betty Union."

Lily saw nothing more of Alice during that afternoon, for she remained in the parlour with her mother, and Lily had to sit upstairs and finish a quantity of needlework which Mrs. Heslope had sent her to do. The day was beautiful and bright, and she longed to take a little walk and breathe the fresh air, but it was in vain to think of doing so, the task set her was so long that it required great diligence to finish it by supper-time, when Mrs. Heslope would expect it to be brought to her. In her former bedroom, of which Alice had now possession, there was a nice, large window, out of which she could see the surrounding country, with the distant hills in the background and magnificent trees in the foreground, and in which she could hear the happy little birds singing, as if thanking God for their bright existence; but the miserable window of her present room was so small and high up, that she could see nothing at all without standing on tiptoe, and even then there was nothing pretty to be seen—no view of the country, no trees, nothing but the stableyard in front and a dirty, muddy pond behind. So poor little Lily felt quite as if she were in prison. She remembered the words of Phœbe, and she tried her best to be cheerful, but yet, despite all her efforts, the tears would trickle down her thin, pale cheeks, and fall on to her hand, and make the needle so sticky that she could not work as fast as she wished, but there was no help for it. She did feel so sad, so lonely, so desolate, poor child; and she thought, too, of the little robin redbreast which used to come to the window to be fed with crumbs which she saved from her breakfast; she felt sure the tame bird would come, and Alice would not feed it, and that it would be so disappointed, and perhaps get starved in the winter. But notwithstanding these sad thoughts she continued to work, stitch, stitch, for almost two hours, at the end of which time she saw the kind face of Phœbe smiling at her door, who said—

"I could not come to you sooner, my dear, for I was obliged to unpack and put away all Miss Alice's clothes (she is always to be called Miss Alice now). She has lots of smart frocks, blue, red, white, lilac and green, and after I had arranged everything in her room she came with her mother to look at it, and she did not even say 'Thank you,' although I had put her things tidy and neat, and have known her since she was a baby. So you see, my child, that you are not the only person who gets treated with unkindness. I could have cried with vexation at her ingratitude, but, fortunately, I remembered that in the morning, when I first got up, I offered everything I might have to do or to suffer during the day to our Lord. I promised to do everything to please Him, therefore that if I did all right, it mattered not whether I was thanked or praised by others. This thought made me quite cheerful again, I merely smiled as I left the room, and said, 'If you require anything more to be done, Miss Alice, call me, I will come and do it.' Neither Alice nor her mother took the trouble of answering me, so I went downstairs where they had been having some tea and bread and butter. I found there was still some warm tea in the pot, and a slice of bread and butter left, so I poured out a nice cup before I cleared the rest away, and I have brought it up to you, my dear, as I am sure you must be thirsty and hungry, and the supper will not be until rather late to-night."

"Oh, thank you, dear Phœbe, how good and kind you are. I am indeed both thirsty and tired, and oh! so sad."

"Of course, you are, my dear, just now, but brisk up, drink this nice, warm tea, and whilst you are refreshing yourself I will get your work on; I can sit here quietly for a bit, as Mrs. Heslope and Miss Alice are gone out for a walk—they are probably gone to meet Mr. Heslope, and they will return home with him in his gig."

The smiles and kind words of Phœbe quite cheered up little Lily, she began to laugh and talk too, and the needlework went on so briskly that it was soon finished off, and Phœbe then told her to put on her hat and go into the garden for a quarter of an hour, as the air would refresh and do her much good. She followed this advice with great pleasure.

It may seem almost unnatural to many

persons that a simple, uneducated servant like Phœbe should have such pious thoughts, or give such sensible advice, but she had enjoyed many advantages when a child, of which she had made good use. Her parents resided close to a convent in Ireland, and she was sent daily to their poor school for some years. One of the nuns' had taken a particular interest in the child on account of her very pious disposition, and frequently gave her extra religious instructions. Many a happy half hour did Phœbe spend in the little parlour of the convent with this good nun; and when she left school, and commenced life in small rough situations, her mind and heart were filled with religious ideas, which she turned to good account in the various troubles which she met with everywhere, but more especially at Mrs. Heslope's.

Phœbe was quite right in thinking that her mistress and Alice had left the house with the intention of taking a pleasant walk, meeting Mr. Heslope, and returning home with him in his gig; but neither mother nor daughter had given a thought to the poor child who was left working upstairs, to whom a little fresh air and exercise would have been so beneficial, they thought of nothing but their own pleasure and enjoyment.

After walking about two miles the gig, with Mr. Heslope in it, appeared in the distance; he saw them coming, urged on his horse a little, and in a few moments was by their side. He jumped out, and gave his daughter a good jolly kiss on each of her fat high-coloured cheeks, which she did not return, but exclaimed in a disdainful tone—

"Law, father, how rough you are, and your face is so prickly, I am sure you have not shaved for a week, at least,—no, I'll not kiss you, indeed, I'm not going to have my face marked more than it is already with your nasty beard."

"I fear you are grown very fine and fanciful, Alice," said her father in a displeased tone; "but it is useless to ape the fine lady here, you will have no one to show off your airs and graces to, I can assure you. How did you leave your aunt? well, I hope?"

"Oh! she was well enough, I believe. Of course she always finds something to complain of, but that is because she is an old maid! and must have something to fidget about. I wouldn't be an old maid for all in the world; I would sooner marry a man with a red nose like 'Billy Lymn.' But of course I shall marry a rich, handsome young man."

"I think you talk a great deal of nonsense, Alice. I am afraid the new friends I have heard so much about have done you harm, and filled your head with vanity; but (turning to his wife) why did you not bring Lily, likewise, with you? the walk and drive would have done her good this fine afternoon, and there is plenty of room for four persons in my gig."

"I left Lily at home," answered Mrs. Heslope, "because she is so idle and careless, she had not half finished her work."

"Has Alice seen her yet."

"Oh yes, pa, she soon found her way into the parlour to have a stare at me."

"I hope you spoke kindly to her, my dear Alice, for she is very timid."

"I said a few words to her, pa, but not much, she looks so stupid—I hate stupid girls."

"She is not stupid, my dear, but she is very timid. She is far from stupid, she reads and writes much better than you did at her age; but you must promise me to be very kind to her."

"All right, pa, all right; now don't bother any more about her; I never cared much for any one, so I am sure not to care much for her."

"Whether you care for her or not, my dear, I cannot help; but I insist on this, that you are neither rude or unkind to her."

"All right, pa, all right, now that's enough about her; tell us what you have done in town."

"Well, I do not think that will interest you much; I bought some flour, a cow, and three pigs."

"No, I don't care a scrap about that; I thought you might have looked in at the shop windows and seen some pretty bonnets, and perhaps have bought me one."

"No, child, I do not care for such things; if your dress is clean and neat, that is enough for me. I should like the hat you have on far better without so many flowers."

"That's because you know nothing of fashions, pa; this is the way girls of my age in Paris have their hats trimmed, and Madame Clarita says it just suits my face; the truth is, you've no taste, pa."

"No, none at all," interposed Mrs. Heslope; "I think Alice looks charming in this hat."

Mr. Heslope said no more, and his pony trotted on so briskly that they very soon reached home, and he immediately called Lily and said to her—

"Here is Alice, my dear; I hope you will be very happy now, with her for a companion in everything; and as she is older than you, she will of course help you in all you have to do. Shake hands, my dears, and let me see you merry together."

Lily held out her hand, and looked beseechingly at Alice, who from fear of her father took the proffered hand, but give it such a pinch that poor Lily started and drew back her hand as quickly as she could.

"What is the matter?" said Mr. Heslope; Lily did not venture a reply, but Alice quickly answered—

"I suppose I did not shake her hand softly enough; what a milksop she must be, as if a touch like that could hurt any one."

"She is not accustomed to such rough fun, Alice, but of course she must not make a fuss about trifles; when she has been with you a short time, she will understand jokes."

" Yes, yes, that she shall," whispered Alice to

her mother; "I'll harden her a bit, see if I don't, in double quick time."

In the evening, Lily read a little as usual to Mr. Heslope, and likewise wrote a few sentences which he read out of a book, in order to teach her writing and spelling at the same time. He told Alice that as she was tired with her journey, she might have a holiday that evening, but that in future he should expect her also to read and write, that he might judge what progress she had made during her three years' residence with her aunt.

She looked very cross, and replied quickly, "Well, I did think that now I am fourteen, there would have been an end of stupid lessons in the evening."

"That must depend on yourself, my dear," said Mr. Heslope; "if I find that you read fluently, write a clear hand, spell correctly, and can run up an account quickly, I shall be quite content. I have no wish for you to be over educated; we shall see to-morrow what you can do."

CHAPTER VII.

TROUBLES WITH ALICE.

THE next morning Lily arose at her usual early hour, and was going downstairs quietly to dust the parlour and make it tidy, when she heard Alice, who was still in bed, calling out loudly—

"I say, Betty Union, 'stir your stumps' a little quicker, and go to the kitchen and fetch me some hot water."

"But there is no fire, Miss Alice, so the water in the boiler is cold."

"Then light the fire, you stupid! and make haste. And take down my shoes to clean too, Betty Union. Mind you're to obey me in everything, for I am Miss Heslope, and you are Miss Nobody—nobody at all, for I have no doubt that your mother was nothing but a tramp—a swing-kettle."

Poor little Lily scarcely understood the meaning of these words, although she felt sure that something ill-natured was intended ; but she obeyed the order thus ungraciously given, went into the kitchen, lighted the fire, and in due time brought a jug of hot water to Alice, who was still lying half asleep lazily in bed. She put the jug on the washhand-stand, and was going away quickly to dust the parlour and do the work Mrs. Heslope required to be finished before breakfast, when she was stopped by shouts from Alice, who bawled out—

"I say, Betty Union, take down my shoes and clean them ; and mind you make them black and glossy and smart."

Lily returned and endeavoured to explain to Alice that Mrs. Heslope expected her to dust the parlour, and would be displeased if it was not finished before breakfast; that as she had already lost much time in lighting the fire to heat the water that she really could not clean her boots then, but would do so directly after breakfast. The only reply was—

"All fudge! All laziness, Betty Union. If you do not take my boots and clean them at once, I'll chuck 'em at your head, depend upon it. I promised to harden you, and I shall begin by your head."

Alice looked so cross, so spiteful, that poor Lily could not venture another word, but took the boots, cleaned, and returned them to Alice, who merely said, "You stupid Betty, you can do nothing well; how badly these boots are cleaned."

"Indeed, I did my best, Miss Alice."

"Then bad is your best, Miss Union. Now, put all the things on my table tidy, hang the cloak on the peg, and put my hat in the hat-box."

Lily obeyed, and put away all the articles which lazy Alice had tossed to and fro in the room to save herself trouble.

Presently, Mrs. Heslope came into the room. She approached Alice's bed, but far from reproaching her with idleness, she merely said—

"What, darling, still in bed! I hope you are rested after your long journey?"

"Oh yes, ma, I'm all right this morning."

"But make haste and get up, darling, or your father will be in a fidget if you are late for breakfast."

Then Mrs. Heslope turned sharply towards

Lily, who was still occupied in tidying things, and said—

"What are you doing here, you slut? have you finished dusting and cleaning the parlour?"

"No, madam, I have not had time," and Lily looked beseechingly at Alice, hoping she would speak for her and tell the truth, but Alice was silent.

"Why have you not finished the parlour?" again demanded Mrs. Heslope with an ominous frown.

Lily cast an imploring look at Alice, and replied, "Miss Alice gave me so many things to do."

Mrs. Heslope looked at Alice, who said—

"I gave her two or three little things to do, but not much. She might have found plenty of time to finish the parlour, but she is such a dawdle."

"That she is, indeed," replied Mrs. Heslope, giving Lily a box on the ear; "take that, and be off at once; and not a bit of breakfast shall you have until the parlour is quite clean and tidy."

Lily left the room as quickly as possible and went downstairs. She knew how much there was to be done in the parlour, which had been used until a late hour the night before, but what was her relief and gratitude to find that good Phœbe, seeing how the case was, had found time to go and dust and arrange everything, so that there was really little or nothing for her to do; that little she did quickly, and then laid the cloth and set everything ready for breakfast.

Just when she had finished, Mr. Heslope came in, and spoke so kindly to her that her spirits revived somewhat; and she reflected with gratitude that if Mrs. Heslope and Alice were ill-natured, that Mr. Heslope and Phœbe were as kind as possible.

Mrs. Heslope soon made the breakfast, and they all sat down; even Alice arrived a few minutes after they had commenced.

"You look as if you had only just tumbled out of bed," said Mr. Heslope; "your hair is awfully untidy, you cannot have brushed it for a week."

"No, pa, it's not untidy; it is the fashion to have it, as Miss Pipkin says, *neglyjaid.*"

"*Neglyjaid!* what does that mean, Alice? I call your hair untidy and slovenly,—very like my old doormat."

F

"O pa! you know nothing about the fashion."

"No, child, nor do I care to know anything. I only wish you would turn your mind to better and more useful things."

Alice did not reply, but looked as sulky as possible, and turned up her nose scornfully.

Mr. Heslope was not easily roused to anger, but her impertinent look and gesture made him really so on this occasion. He turned to her sternly and said—

"If you could see your own face, Alice, you would be perfectly ashamed. Your nose is not handsome at any time, but when you turn it up in that unbecoming manner, you make your face quite frightful."

"That's not true, pa, my nose is not frightful. Miss Pipkin, who has been in Paris, says it is what they call there '*ratrussade*,' and it gives my face a '*piccant*' look."

"How can you talk such absurd nonsense, Alice, and believe all those silly girls tell you?"

"You're so cross, pa,—I wish I'd not come home at all."

"Well, Alice, we can soon settle that matter; for unless you behave better I will send you to a boarding-school in Llanarth, where the girls are kept under such strict discipline that (to use a common expression) they scarcely dare say their soul is their own. It is kept by Mrs. Middleton and her sister Miss Crate. Such a school would, I am sure, do you all the good in the world; and I give you fair notice that if ever again you answer me and behave in such an unbecoming manner, that I shall send you off there at once."

Mr. Heslope rose from his seat as he said these words, and left the room ; but he had effectually alarmed both mother and daughter, for they had heard of this school, and they both knew well that if Mr. Heslope once really determined on a matter, he was certain to be as good as his word.

So they looked at one another, and Alice began to cry and exclaim between her sobs—

" How cross and disagreeable pa is; I wish there was not a papa in the whole world."

These words filled little Lily with astonishment, as the one wish of her heart, and her one daily prayer was, that she might some day be restored to her own dear father. Unconsciously to herself she gave a sudden start, and looked up. Both mother and daughter had forgotten her presence, but her look reminded them that they were not alone; and they immediately vented their wrath on the poor unoffending child.

"What are you dawdling over your breakfast and losing your time for?" said Mrs. Heslope, giving Lily an impatient shove. "Be off at once and do your work, you lost time enough this morning."

"Yes," chimed in Alice; "go and make my bed, Betty Union."

Lily left the room quickly, and the mother and daughter began to talk over the matter of Mr. Heslope's displeasure.

"You must, at least, pretend to do as he wishes, darling," said Mrs. Heslope; "I know he is very cross and disagreeable. I suffer enough from it at times, but there's no help for it, he is the master, and if he once makes up his mind to send you to that school, he'll do it, as sure as I'm alive."

"But I wouldn't stay there, I'd run away, mother, and tell no one who I was; and then pa would be frightened, and think I was dead."

"But where could you run to, my darling? If you ran out into the woods you would be

starved, and if you ran into the town, and would
not tell the magistrates who you were, you
would be sent off to the union, or a reformatory,
and you would not like that; and I should die
of grief if I heard you were missing. No, you'd
best be quiet and civil with your pa, and in a
short time you'll be a woman, and then you'll
marry some one (not an old crosspatch like
your father, but some goodnatured, rich man),
and then you can dress just as you please; so
now make up your mind not to aggravate your
pa, if you can possibly help it."

"Well, mother, I'll see what I can do, for I
shouldn't like the union a bit better than Mrs.
Middleton's, and a reformatory would be worse
still. But I do so hate the idea of doing lessons
in the evening with that Betty Union. Does she
read and write well, mother, better than I?"

"Your father says so, but then he thinks
that she does everything well, just because he
fancies her mother was some fine lady, married
to some fine gentleman, so you must be civil to
her whenever he is anywhere near."

"Yes, I'll be civil enough when he is near, but
I'll pay her off whenever he is away. I hate the
girl, with her smooth face, and hair plastered

down as if it was glued to her head. I'll give her a cold pig some day, to see if I can wash the varnish off."

"How full of fun you are, my dear child, and your eyes look as bright as diamonds."

"Oh yes, mother, Miss Pipkin says I have melting eyes. I do not understand exactly what that means, but I am sure by her smile that she meant something very beautiful. I remember her saying this last Christmas, just after I had given her one of the delicious mince-pies you sent me in the basket with the fat turkey. I showed her the turkey, and told her she should have a bit, and she kissed me on both cheeks; but I forgot all about it. She promised me some ear-rings before I returned home; but she never sent them, although I reminded her very often."

"That was provoking," said Mrs. Heslope; "but you need not mind, for I know that your father has a beautiful pair for you, that his mother wore when she was married."

"But they must be as old-fashioned as the hills. I'll not wear such things if he gives them to me; so I hope he won't, every one would suppose that I came out of the Ark."

"If he offers them to you, darling, I advise you to accept them, not to refuse his gift; you need only wear them when no one is here, that can do no harm, and will satisfy him."

"Yes, and when I am married I will change them quickly enough for something else. But I hear pa coming, so I shall go upstairs, and I hope he will be in a better skin when I come to dinner."

Mr. Heslope entered the parlour, and asked where Lily and Alice were gone. He was told that both were upstairs busily employed, which satisfied him. True enough it was that Lily was busily employed; Mrs. Heslope and Alice took care that she should have no idle time; but as for Alice she spent the greatest part of the morning lolling in an arm-chair, reading a love-tale she had purchased second-hand at a book stall.

Mr. Heslope said a few words to his wife about the impertinence of Alice; but she only laughed and said he was a great fool for expecting to find an old head on young shoulders; but that Alice was determined to try and be more steady and staid in future, therefore he must say no more on the matter.

"I hope this is true," answered Mr. Heslope; "how happy should I be if I really saw her make efforts to improve, but I hardly dare hope such a thing, although I shall say no more to her at present, and I hope and trust that she will, at least, endeavour to keep her promise."

At dinner-time Mr. Heslope spoke in his usually kind tone to Alice; and she was glad to find that he said no more about Mrs. Middleton's school.

CHAPTER VIII.

ALICE'S IGNORANCE.

ON the evening of the second day after the arrival of Alice, after supper she endeavoured to slip out of the room unperceived, and ran upstairs hoping to escape what she called the "nasty lessons" with her father; he, however, soon called her downstairs again, and said she must make up her mind to devote the evening to reading and writing.

"I should like, my dear, in the first place, to see whether you are improved in your writing and spelling, so write a letter to your aunt to tell her that you arrived here safely, and found your mother and myself well; write it nicely, and I will send it to her to-morrow."

"No, pa, I hate writing to aunt, she always laughs at my letters, even when I have taken pains in writing them, and makes game of me."

"Then try, my dear, to write such a nice letter that there may be nothing to laugh at in it;

begin at once, child, do not lose any more time disputing."

So Alice was obliged to commence. She wrote very slowly, and very badly too, but blamed everything save herself—the ink she said was thick, the paper too thin, and the pen so sharp that it made holes in the paper.

At length, however, the letter was said to be finished, and Mr. Heslope took it to read, but no sooner had he read the first lines than he burst into such an uncontrollable fit of laughter that he almost tumbled off his chair, and exclaimed—

"No wonder your aunt laughs at your letters, my dear, no wonder! Who could help doing so? Read this, Mrs. Heslope, see how well your daughter spells," and he gave his wife the following letter to read—

"Deer Ant,

"I got threw my jurnay all right, I was hawful colde, and lost my shew, cos it was so big. Pa, and ma, are whel. There is a new gal hear who pa keaps. I hop you keap whel and no ead-ake. Ma's got bak-ake.

"Ime your fond neace
"ALICE HESLOPE."

Even Mrs. Heslope could scarce prevent a smile at this absurd production, but she merely handed the letter back to Mr. Heslope, and said—

"There are a few mistakes, to be sure, but they can be easily corrected; Alice wrote this in a hurry."

"We will see how that is, my dear," answered Mr. Heslope. "I fear the truth is, that Alice spells as badly now as she did when she left us two years ago, but we will see," he said, returning the letter to his daughter, who was now sitting in a sulky, angry attitude. "I will give you a quarter of an hour, Alice, to sit quietly and correct this letter yourself. If you can do so I shall be pleased, and only recommend you to be more careful in future; but if you cannot, I shall henceforth insist on your doing lessons, as you call it, every evening until I find you can really write a respectable letter, and spell it properly."

"No, I've a headache, pa, I can't do anything more to-night."

"Nonsense, child, you have eaten a good dinner, your cheeks are as rosy as an apple, your headache is a mere sham. Begin correcting your letter at once, begin by the first words, 'Deer ant.'"

"But I am certain they are both quite right, pa, for I've a book of verses that Miss Wireworm gave me, and the first verse is—

> 'See that lovely, gentle deer,
> And those ants so very near.'

Look yourself, pa, here it is," and she pulled out of her pocket a crumpled book of nursery verses, "look at those two words, pa,—deer and ant,—now I'm right and you wrong."

"Did you read the rest of the verse, my dear?"

"Oh no, pa! that would have been too much trouble, but I picked out those two words to put in my letter, as I was not sure about them."

"Well, listen, Alice, and I will read you the two next lines.

> "'See that lovely, gentle deer,
> And those ants so very near ;
> The first has horns and spotted back,
> The last has legs so shiny black.'

"There, Alice! has your aunt horns and a spotted back, or black, shiny legs? If you had read the next lines you would have seen at once that the verse is about those beautiful quadrupeds called deer, which you have seen in parks, and the insect called an ant. If you had been writing to this animal or that insect" (showing her a print of both), "your spelling would have been correct; as it is, it is laughably wrong. Now begin in good earnest, try to correct the rest, and I will look at it in a quarter of an hour, when I have finished hearing Lily read."

Alice took the letter sulkily, and pretended to read it over and correct it, but at the end of a quarter of an hour the only changes made were a few blots, some words scratched out, and the word "deer" changed to "dear,"—as for "ant," although she knew it was wrong, yet she had no idea that the right spelling was "aunt."

Mr. Heslope did not look angry when, at the end of a quarter of an hour, she returned the letter uncorrected, but he spoke in a sorrowful tone, as he said—

"I am indeed grieved, my dear child, to find that you have learned nothing during these two last years, for if your spelling is so bad, of course other things have been equally neglected. You must now make up for lost time, and try to improve as fast as you can during the two hours I shall devote to you, henceforth, in the evening."

Alice did not dare reply, as she felt sure that any attempt at resistance would at once decide Mr. Heslope to send her off to Mrs. Middleton's school, which she really dreaded.

Mrs. Heslope was much annoyed and provoked, more especially as Lily was in the room during the whole of this laughable scene, and she felt sure that the child would rejoice at the humiliation of her daughter. She was, however, quite mistaken in this idea, for Lily's only thought was that, perhaps, by helping Alice a little in spelling and other things she might gain her love.

But she was, alas! quite disappointed in these hopes, for mortification had not the slightest beneficial effect upon Alice, who, on the following morning, was more cross and domineering than ever, and ordered her about here and there, first for one thing, then another, so that she could not possibly get through her work. And when she was scolded by Mrs. Heslope for idleness, Alice quite rejoiced, and was never honourable enough to tell her mother the real cause of the work not being finished before breakfast.

Phœbe was seldom able to assist her now, as Mr. Heslope had bought two new cows, and she was obliged to milk them at that hour.

Day after day poor little Lily could not come to breakfast until it was half over, on account of her work not being finished, and Mr. Heslope, who loved regularity, was annoyed. Mrs. Heslope, however, always maintained that the sole cause of all was the idleness of Lily, therefore he was displeased with her, and said nothing when she did come in.

At last, however, he determined to speak to her on the subject himself, as she was usually so obedient and docile that he could not understand such constant neglect of duty; he therefore called her into his room one day, and said—

"What is the reason, Lily, that you are so idle in the morning, and never get your work finished before breakfast? Do you remain in bed after you are called?"

"Oh no, sir! I always get up at six o'clock, directly the bell rings."

"Then how is it that your work is not finished?"

"If you please, sir, I have so much to do for Miss Alice that I have not time. I have to light the fire to warm water for her, then I have to clean her boots and shoes, then to tidy her room, and when all that is done, she finds numbers of other things for me to do, darning her stockings and mending her clothes. Often she does not let me leave her room until almost eight o'clock, then of course I have no time to clean the parlour, but she does not care for that; only do not, if you please, sir, let Mrs. Heslope know that I told you all this, she would be so angry."

"Do not be afraid, my dear, I will not betray you, and you have only told me the truth because I questioned you; but does Mrs. Heslope really know that Alice prevents your doing your work?"

"I think not, sir, for she will not listen to a word I say in explanation, and Miss Alice will not say anything to excuse me."

"Very well, my dear, I will try what I can do to help you, and I will be most careful not to let any one know that you have told me these things, but you must not speak about it yourself."

"I assure you, sir, that there is no fear of my telling Mrs. Heslope or Alice anything, for they never talk to me; and if I told Phœbe, she is so good and kind that she would not say anything that might get me scolded."

"Very well, my dear, now run away and do your work; I will see what I can do to help you."

He said this with a smile, but the smile did not come from his heart; his heart was sad, sad beyond expression, for he was so grieved at the behaviour of his wife and daughter to the poor and unprotected little girl. He did not doubt the truth of what she had told him, as he had never detected her in the slightest lie, and he could not bear to think of the treatment she had received in his house. He determined to keep a good look-out in the morning, and then judge from what he remarked himself how to act in the matter.

Usually Farmer Heslope went to his farm and stables from six o'clock in the morning until the breakfast-time, eight o'clock, but as on the following morning he expected a load of corn he had purchased to be brought in, that would form a sufficient reason for remaining at home without exciting suspicion, in order to make arrangements for storing it away in his outhouses. But he said nothing on the subject to his wife or Alice, lest the idea of his being at home should put the latter on her guard, and prevent her acting as usual.

He arose at his usual hour, and at six o'clock heard Mrs. Heslope ring the old cracked bell to rouse Phœbe from her heavy slumbers, and likewise to call Lily. He heard the latter get up instantly, and begin to dress without a moment's delay. She left her room at half-past six, after having made her bed, and went quietly downstairs to light the kitchen fire in order to put on the kettle to warm water for Alice, and it was very long before she succeeded in lighting it as the sticks were green and wet.

Long before this was accomplished he heard the shrill voice of his daughter vociferating—

"I say, Betty Union, be quick; bring my water."

"The kettle does not boil yet, Miss Alice."

"Oh, you lazybones, how long you have been lighting the fire."

"The sticks were green, miss, I could not light it."

"Stuff and nonsense! you did not try."

At last the kettle boiled, and Lily carried up the water and entered Alice's room.

"There, put it down quick, you stupid Union. Now, take my two pair of boots to clean, sew on the buttons where they are come off, and then come and tidy this room, Betty, or you shall have the worst of it, you may depend."

"I will make all the haste I can, miss, but I am sure I shall not then have time to do the parlour before breakfast, as it is almost half-past seven."

"I do not care in the least whether it is done or not, but you do what I bid you at once."

The poor child obeyed, and at five minutes to eight was still in Alice's room. She then let her go down, lest her father should come in, but it was, of course, impossible for Lily to clean and tidy a room in five minutes, therefore when Mrs. Heslope entered it, there was the usual scene of scolding and threats. The poor child was not allowed to say one word in self-defence, but was sentenced to finish everything before she came to breakfast, so that all had done their breakfast before she entered, and Mrs. Heslope was in such a hurry to clear everything away that Lily had scarcely time to eat a mouthful.

When she had finished her scanty portion and left the room, Mr. Heslope told his wife and daughter to remain, as he wished to speak to them both, and he thus addressed the latter—

"I heard you this morning shouting out in a loud tone from your bed, 'Betty Union, Betty Union!' Now, I should like to know who you designate by that elegant name?"

Alice got very red, fidgeted about in her chair, seemed anxious to get up and go away to evade further questions, and said to her mother—

"O ma! I quite forgot to bring in the basket of cakes you told me to put in the cupboard; I must run and fetch them at once, or I fear that Nelson, who was unchained a few minutes ago, will find them and gobble them up."

But Mr. Heslope said in a stern tone—

"Sit still, Alice, remain where you are, never mind the cakes, but answer my question at once, Who is Betty Union?"

"Why, pa, you know very well that Betty

and Bet are the short for Elizabeth; all Elizabeths are called Betty or Bet, so I call Lily Betty. It's my fun, nothing but fun, she doesn't care about it a bit."

" Have you ever asked her?"

"No, pa; but of course she doesn't mind such a bit of fun."

"I will not ask you the meaning of adding the word *Union* to Betty. I see too plainly your cruel, derisive meaning, and I grieve from my heart to think that I have a child capable of thus deriding the sorrows of a poor, unoffending, unprotected fellow-creature. You may well cry, Alice, but I fear that your tears are merely the tears of mortified pride. I could cry, too, I can assure you, but I grieve because you do not grieve, and thus show a complete want of heart. I heard everything that took place in your room this morning. I now know how you employ the time of poor Lily in the morning, first in lighting the fire and heating water for you, then in cleaning your shoes, arranging your untidy room, and a thousand other things that you ought to do yourself, instead of remaining indolently in bed. You did not allow her to leave your room until five minutes to eight, how was it possible for her to clean a room out in that time? and each day you have had the cruelty to let the poor girl be scolded and punished for a fault which you alone had occasioned. I am ashamed of your conduct, Alice, indeed I am."

"You are so cross, pa; you always find fault with me for everything I do or say. I believe you hate me, I am quite sure you do, you only care for that odious Lil, whom I detest every day more and more. I should like to kill her, and myself too."

As Alice said these words she burst into a passion of tears and sobs, and tumbled off her chair on to the floor, where she remained kicking and gasping and pretending to be dying, in hopes of frightening her father. But he sat still and stern, and would not allow Mrs. Heslope to approach her daughter, as he well knew that she would begin to pet and console her, which he did not wish. So Alice continued to sob and groan, but at last, finding no one noticed her, that her demonstrations of despair were totally unheeded, she got up, sat again on her chair, and turned her face away from her father, who then spoke—

"My dear Alice (for dear you are to me, notwithstanding all your faults), listen to me, and remember that if you presume to disobey my commands instant and severe punishment shall follow. From this day forward I forbid you to call that poor girl by any name but her own, Lily, neither Betty nor Bet, nor, above all, 'Union.' I forbid you to order her, henceforth, to do the slightest thing for you. If you require hot water, get up a little earlier, light the fire, and boil it for yourself; clean your own boots, sweep your own room, and we shall see henceforth whether Lily does not easily complete her own work before breakfast, when not called away to wait on you. And now you may go away as soon as you please."

Alice arose from her seat and went out of the room without uttering a word. She was thoroughly humbled, but, alas! had not the slightest feeling of grief, excepting for the mortification she had brought on herself.

As soon as she was gone Mrs. Heslope endeavoured to excuse her, and talked of the folly of expecting to find "old heads on young shoulders," but Mr. Heslope silenced her by saying, in a sorrowful tone—

"No more on that subject, if you please."

Although Lily's position in the family was a little improved by the firmness displayed by Mr. Heslope, yet she was still very, very unhappy; for neither Mrs. Heslope nor Alice ever let pass an opportunity of saying or doing anything unkind in her regard, and Alice was jealous, too, because Lily read, wrote, and spelt so much better than herself, although she was obliged to keep silence on the subject when in the presence of her father. He seldom praised Lily, lest it should arouse angry feelings in the heart of his daughter and her mother, but in his own mind he was often astonished at the facility with which she learned everything as also at her intuitive shrinking from all that approached in the slightest degree to coarseness or vulgarity. He frequently sighed when he compared her to his own child.

The only fault for which he had ever reason to reprove Lily was a want of tidiness, her books were so often dirtied and torn, and there were constantly blots and stains on her copybook. She could not account for these blemishes, she never remembered how they were done, but yet there they were, so she was of course blamed; no one else could have blotted her book or made smears on the writing, as her things were never left about the room, but always put carefully in her desk each evening after she had used them. Her desk was quite small, and she kept it in a large drawer in an old table that stood in the corner; neither desk nor drawer had any key, but that did not signify, as no one but herself used that table or that drawer. She promised Mr. Heslope every evening to be more careful, but yet the same untidy books with great blots in them, as if shut up in a hurry, appeared over and over again; so that at last he was really displeased and spoke quite sharply to her several times on the subject, which distressed her very much, as she really loved him and wished to please him.

CHAPTER IX.

LILY LOSES HER ONLY FRIEND.

TIME went on, but one morning Phœbe came into Lily's room with tears in her eyes, but apparently unable to speak.

"What is the matter, dear Phœbe? what can be the matter?" exclaimed Lily in alarm. "Oh, do tell me!"

But Phœbe did not reply, her heart seemed so full as totally to prevent utterance, but at last she faltered out these words—

"My poor dear mother in Ireland is very, very ill, and she told Phelim O'Connor (the boy she adopted when his mother died) to write and beg me to return home without delay, as she has no one to nurse her, and she lives at a great distance from any town."

"Oh, dear Phœbe! and must you really go? Do take me with you. What shall I do without you, you my only friend."

"My child, it would be impossible for me to take you with me, Mr. Heslope would not allow it, and I live in such an unfrequented part of Ireland that you would lose all chance of being ever found by your father. Now, here you have some chance, for so many travellers come and go, and Mr. Heslope tells your history to many and begs them to do what they can to help him find your father, that you may be restored to your family; so you cannot leave."

"That is true, dear Phœbe, I heard him yesterday talking to the gentleman who had that beautiful horse, and came here for fishing; unhappy as I am, I must not give up all hopes of finding my dear father. But how soon shall you be obliged to go?"

"I must not delay long, my dear, for my mother has no one to look after her but Phelim, and he is in the fields all day working. You know that my only sister married a year and a half ago, and emigrated with her husband to America."

"But you will write to me, Phœbe, when you are gone, will you not? Oh, how sad and lonely I shall be without you."

"Yes, yes, I will write, but my mother lives

in such an unfrequented part of Ireland, that I shall not often be able to post a letter."

When Phœbe left the room poor Lily sat down and cried very bitterly at the thought of losing her only friend, but she cast a look on her little crucifix, and that look recalled to her mind words once said by her mother to a person in grief, which she, child as she was, had listened to and remembered—

"When you feel very sad and very lonely, think of our Lord hanging on the cross; put your sorrows at His feet, ask Him to help you."

She was too young to comprehend the words at that time, but now she had had so much sorrow that she quite understood where she was to go for consolation, and she begged our Lord to help her, and a feeling of peace and calm came over the poor child, and her tears fell with less bitterness, but yet to lose her only friend was a sad grief. She thought how she should now be without any one to whom she could tell her many trials, with no one to give her advice, with no one to love her,—the tears continued to chase one another down her pale cheeks, but she was silent.

Lily saw nothing more of Phœbe during that

day, for the time of the latter was fully occupied by Mrs. Heslope, who insisted on her washing and cleaning up everything in the house before she left.

Phœbe obeyed, and obeyed willingly, as she felt certain that anything she omitted doing would fall to the lot of poor little Lily, for Alice did nothing, and a new servant could not be got at once. It was quite late in the evening, when Lily was gone up to bed, that Phœbe's work was finished, and she managed to spare half an hour to talk to the poor child. She gave her a great deal of good, pious, sensible advice on all points, and recommended her to take the greatest possible care of the miniature of her father, as it might some day be the means of her discovering him.

As the miniature was very small, she advised her always to keep it inside the lining of her stays, not let Alice see it on any account, and never speak of it. Mrs. Heslope had most probably quite forgotten its existence, but if seen by either of them they would most likely insist on selling it, as the jewels of the setting might be worth something, and they would sell it even for a few shillings.

Lily promised to be most careful in this respect, and Phœbe then said a few words more on patience in her trials, on trust in God alone, and on regularity in her religious duties.

"It is seldom, I know," said Phœbe, "that you can get to mass on account of the distance, *that* has been my greatest trial here, but things in that respect may get better after a time. You must put your trust in God, and be certain that He will take care of you, that if He does allow trials to come upon you He sees that they are necessary, and that they will bring you to a bright crown in heaven. You are too young to understand all this now, but some day you will, and then you will thank God gratefully for every cross He has sent you in this world."

Lily promised to remember all Phœbe's advice, and to follow it carefully.

"And now, my dear," said Phœbe, "you shall see the little parting present I have brought you—I purchased it from a poor boy. I thought it might amuse and interest you when I am gone, and you have no one to talk to, for you can love and pet it."

As Phœbe said these words she produced

from under her apron a small box, which she opened, and Lily saw in it a pretty little dormouse nestled up in some moss and leaves.

"Oh! what a sweet little mouse," said Lily, in great delight, "what lovely eyes it has, what beautiful soft hair, and such a nice long tail, too. But will it ever get to know me and to love me?"

"Yes," answered Phœbe; "if you feed it yourself and take care of it, it will soon know and get fond of you. You can let it out of its cage when you are alone, it will amuse you to see all its gambols when you are working. You must save little bits to feed it with at dinner and supper, and in the summer, when there are plenty of apples in the orchard, you can pick up one occasionally for it. But you must be most careful about the cat, as it would eat your mouse in two minutes; and you must never let it be out of the box when you are not in the room, as it might run out and go downstairs, and you may be certain that Mrs. Heslope would kill it if she saw it, as she hates mice, and would not believe that this is not a common mouse."

"I will take such care of my mouse, dear Phœbe, thank you so much for it."

"And now, dear child, I must say good-bye, as I am going away very early in the morning. Bill Slade will drive me to the inn where I shall meet the stage-coach."

"But you must write to me directly you reach home, Phœbe! You will not forget?"

"Oh no, I will not forget, and you must write to me as often as you can. Good-bye, my poor child, may God bless and take care of you."

Phœbe rushed out of the room as she said these words; her heart was too full to say more. Lily did not dare follow lest she should meet Mrs. Heslope, but she went to bed and cried herself to sleep.

She awoke next morning with a heavy heart, and could scarcely bring herself to the comprehension that she was really going to lose her only friend and comforter. She crept out of her room in hopes of seeing Phœbe once more, but found, alas! that she was gone, had been gone full half-an-hour. She had looked into her room as she passed, and would not waken the poor child sooner than was necessary.

Oh! how desolate and lonely poor Lily felt she reflected that her only friend was gone, that there was no one now to help her, or give her a kind word of encouragement.

She sat and thought of her sorrows, and felt as if she could not exert herself to dress and do her work, when suddenly she was aroused by hearing a slight scratching sound. She started, and remembered the mouse; this thought calmed her sadness for the moment. She immediately went to the box, gave it some food, and made it clean and comfortable, and put it up in a safe place before she went downstairs.

At the end of the week she wrote a long letter to Phœbe, as she had promised, and gave it to the stable-boy to post when he went to market at the town where the post-office was.

She expected each day to hear from Phœbe, but no letter came. Mrs. Heslope had made up her mind to stop all communication between them, as she said that Phœbe made a fool of the child, and prevented her doing her work properly. Therefore Alice, who delighted in anything ill-natured, managed somehow to get possession of every letter and immediately consigned it to the fire. She took a malicious pleasure in teasing poor Lily about not getting a letter, and said constantly in a jeering tone—

"How many letters have you had from your friend Phœbe?"

And when Lily was obliged to acknowledge that she had not heard even once, Mrs. Heslope would exclaim in a scornful tone—

"Of course not, you are very stupid to expect letters from her. She has plenty to do without wasting time in writing to you; she has quite forgotten you, depend upon it."

These, and such like words cut Lily to the heart. She did not believe that Phœbe had forgotten her, but yet she could not understand her letters being all left unanswered. The idea of their having been stopped and burned, never once entered her simple, unsuspicious mind, but the feeling of loneliness was increased tenfold. The only pleasure the poor child had was her mouse,—she loved it almost as the poor prisoner loved his tame rat; but even her pleasure with the mouse was embittered by the fear lest Mrs. Heslope or Alice should discover that she had it. They both pretended to have the greatest fear of a mouse, and would certainly, if they saw it, insist on its being killed at once.

CHAPTER X.

FRESH SORROWS ARISE.

MR. HESLOPE continued for many months to give instructions to the two girls every evening. He had had a good plain education himself, and having much natural ability was well calculated for teaching; and as he had the greatest horror of an ignorant, uneducated woman, he took immense pains with Alice, and would not listen to her constant request for a holiday on account of some fancied headache or toothache, or fatigue from a walk.

Lily delighted in learning quite as much as Alice detested it; and Mr. Heslope frequently sighed when he contrasted the talent and industry of Lily, with the dull intellect and sullen inattention of his own daughter, but he never dared praise Lily for fear of arousing the jealous feelings of Alice, therefore the "lesson time," as she called it, went on each evening quietly.

It was the only happy hour in the day for little Lily,—the rest of her time, in the absence of Mr. Heslope, was passed in a constant series of scolding and hard work.

Time passed on, drearily, wearily, for poor Lily; there was no change in the sad monotony of her existence, and she began to despair of ever having the one happiness she sighed for,— the happiness of finding her father. One day, however, she was aroused and frightened by hearing a neighbour say—

"How ill Mr. Heslope looks, and he seems so dull and out of spirits, too; what can be the matter?"

Lily had thought many times that he looked ill and dull, but the words of the neighbour made her think more seriously on the matter; and it was not until she was thus alarmed that she felt how much she loved him for his constant kindness, and how his loss would be the loss of everything to her, so she began to watch every movement with anxiety.

Her anxiety was not without reason; he was both ill and depressed, and the cause of his low spirits was pecuniary distress, brought on, in the first place, by loss of visitors at his inn, which defalcation was occasioned by the establishment of a grand new-fashioned hotel, within a few miles of his own, which attracted some of his oldest and best customers; secondly, by the extravagance of Mrs. Heslope and Alice. When he complained and entreated them to be more careful, the answer he invariably received from one and the other was—

"You must be rich; if you were not, you would soon give up keeping a beggar girl. Do not suppose that we shall either of us take the trouble of saving money just for you to spend it on her."

Lily heard these words, which were said in a loud angry tone by Mrs. Heslope; they cut her to the heart, and she longed to go anywhere and to do anything, rather than continue to be such a cause of trouble to her kind benefactor. But where was she to go? What was she to do? that was the question, for she had not a friend in the world now that Phœbe was gone.

One evening Mr. Heslope told the two girls that he was going up to London in the following week on business, and that he would bring each a present if they gave him satisfaction in what he required them to do. Alice was to write a letter of one page in length, without more than six faults in spelling, and Lily was to write a letter of four pages, without one blot or dirty mark.

The girls were delighted at the idea of a present from London, especially as Mr. Heslope gave them leave to make choice of what they pleased. Lily determined, if she succeeded in gaining a prize, to ask for a book, and Alice set her heart on a smart new hat with a white feather; both wrote their letters carefully, and each put their own away in the proper place.

On the following evening after supper, Mr. Heslope said, "Now, Alice, and Lily, bring your letters quickly for me to see, that I may decide whether they are sufficiently well written to merit the prize."

Alice brought hers first; she had taken pains with it, therefore it was better than usual; there were five faults of spelling, it is true, but as six were allowed she had fairly gained her promised reward, and with a face radiant with delight said that she wished for a hat with a white feather in it.

Mr. Heslope would have been better pleased

if his daughter had made choice of something more useful, but as he had promised to purchase whatever she wished for, he at once acceded to her wish.

It was then the turn of Lily to produce her letter; she opened the box where she had put it the night before, took it out, and placed it in the hands of Mr. Heslope. He read the first page and said—

"Very nice, indeed, Lily, and so neat and clean too." But when he turned over the page there was, alas! a great blot of ink on the second sheet, which was smeared in many places over the third. She had apparently dropped some ink from her pen, and not perceiving it, turned over quickly to the fourth, and the second and third pages were stuck together by the drop of ink.

Mr. Heslope looked displeased and said—

"What a pity it is, Lily, that you are not more careful, you have lost your prize."

Poor little Lily could not help crying; she was disappointed at losing her prize, and grieved at having displeased Mr. Heslope. She had not perceived this unfortunate drop of ink, she thought her letter was so nice and clean.

However, there was no help for it now, therefore Mr. Heslope dipped a pen in Alice's inkstand, and told the two girls to write their names in turn at the end of their letters. They did so, and took them to the fire to dry the ink.

Alice dried hers first, and exclaimed in surprise, when she looked at her writing after holding it to the fire for a few minutes—

"O pa! how funny, my writing is turned quite red, as if I had written with red ink instead of black."

"It is a particular kind of ink," said her father; "it has the peculiar property of turning red if it is held to the fire. I filled your bottle with it to surprise you. Now, Lily, dry your writing before you put it away."

Lily did so, and in a moment held up her writing, likewise, in surprise, exclaiming—

"My name and the blots and smears are turned quite red, but the rest of my writing remains black."

She looked at Alice and perceived that her face was become quite as red as the blots. Mr. Heslope, too, looked at the guilty red face of Alice, and said sternly—

"Well may you blush, Alice, at this unexpected discovery of your fraud. Do not attempt to deny it, it must have been you who blotted Lily's letter with ink out of your own bottle, unconscious that your ink was different from hers. I am shocked,—I am grieved at your ill-natured duplicity. Your reward is of course forfeited; and that is a much smaller punishment than you deserve."

Alice tried to say something rude to defend herself, but Mr. Heslope ordered her to leave the room at once and go to bed.

He did not dare say much to Lily, for fear of provoking the wrath of Mrs. Heslope, but he asked what he was to bring for her from London, and she said, "A book, if you please," and then went upstairs to prepare for bed.

Directly she entered her room she went to look at her pet dormouse, but she found the box empty. The little creature, tired of its confinement, had gnawed a hole in the box and escaped. She was terribly undone and hunted for it everywhere, but, unfortunately, in the midst of her search, she knocked down an empty box, and the noise of its fall was heard by Alice, who came upstairs and asked in an angry tone what she was making such a disturbance for? In an unguarded moment she replied that she was looking for her dormouse.

"What dormouse?" said Alice.

"Oh! a pretty little creature which Phœbe gave me before she left, I am so fond of it; I am sure it must be in the room somewhere; do, dear Miss Alice, help me to look for it."

"Oh yes, I'll soon help you to find it," said Alice. She darted out of the room and returned, to the horror of Lily, with the black cat in her arms, and despite the tears and entreaties of the poor child put it down in the room. Lily did her utmost to turn the cat out of the room again; but Alice, who was as strong as a horse, seized, held her hands, and would not let her move. She then pushed Lily on to the bed, kept her there, and made her look on whilst the cat hunted round the room, and finally paused and made a spring at something on the floor in the corner. That something was her poor little mouse, which it killed and eat in two minutes.

Lily ceased struggling and shut her eyes, but she did not say a word, she did not utter a lamentation; she felt that so far from receiving sympathy, that her sorrow would be treated with derision.

Alice said tauntingly, as she left the room—

"Pretty impudence, indeed! to dare keep vermin in my mother's house; try it again, I advise you, Miss Betty Union."

Lily remained sitting on the bed for some time, thinking how she had now lost the only creature which loved her on earth, and her thoughts were sad, oh! very sad. Those who are surrounded with loving friends and pleasures of every description, will smile at her grief, they cannot comprehend her feelings; but "Silvio Pelico" (the unfortunate prisoner who was confined for so many years in dungeons in Italy) would have understood her feelings at once; he would have remembered what he felt when removed suddenly into a different dungeon, and thus deprived of the spider which he had tamed and accustomed to come to him for food.

Lily raised her eyes mechanically and looked around the miserable little room, which now felt far more lonely than ever; her eyes rested on the picture given her by Phœbe, and the sight of it roused her in a degree, and made her remember the advice given at the same time. She knelt down, and the poor desolate child endeavoured to lay her many sorrows at the feet of our Lord, and begged of Him to remove her from a place where she was so miserable. She prayed with simple faith, and then went to her bed silently and sorrowfully.

Notwithstanding her grief, she soon fell asleep, for she was young and very tired, but her dreams were troubled by visions of mice and cats, and unkindness, and ink, and blots.

The next morning she rose and went about her work as usual; Mr. Heslope was gone, and neither Alice nor her mother spoke a word excepting to find fault. She neither attempted to speak or to defend herself, her spirit was utterly broken, she seemed to care for nothing. The inn was, however, unusually filled with travellers on that day, and among others there was a farmer of the name of Brandon, who called to rest for a few hours, as he had been walking a great distance to purchase some sheep which were now being driven to his farm. He complained that from having been obliged to walk so much his stockings were sadly worn and full of holes, and he asked whether it would be possible to find any one to mend them for him during the time he was resting at the inn, and getting his dinner.

Mrs. Heslope instantly called Lily, and desired her to mend the holes in his stockings. She darned extremely well, and took great pains with them, for he smiled so kindly when he gave them to her, saying—

"Do not be frightened, lass, at the big holes. I shall be most thankful if you can sew them up."

Lily took the stockings, worked diligently, and finished darning up every hole in about two hours. She would have liked to take them to the farmer herself, in order to get another kind smile, but Mrs. Heslope snatched them out of her hands, and took them herself.

He was delighted when he looked at them, and saw how nice and strong they were, and exclaimed—

"How I wish I had a lass like that in my house; my three girls are twice as big, but none of them can darn a stocking, or mend anything."

"Do you really mean," said Mrs. Heslope quickly, "that you should like to have this girl for a servant? we should be delighted to get rid of her, she costs so much to keep, and is the cause of constant quarrels between my husband and myself, he makes such a fool of her, and indulges her in everything."

"But will Mr. Heslope be willing to part with her?"

"I do not know, and I do not care. He took her without my leave, and I will part with her without his leave; he will find her gone, and must make the best of it; he can grumble until he is tired, I shall not care so as we get rid of the girl. Do not tell me where you live, for if I do not know he cannot insist on my telling him, which he might do, if I knew anything."

"But will the lass be willing to leave you, and go to live with me, a complete stranger?"

"Of course she will; she will like a change, depend on it, for she has neither gratitude nor affection in her disposition; she has not a scrap of love for my Alice, who has been like a sister to her. But I will call the girl and you shall judge for yourself.

"Lily, come here."

Lily entered the room timidly, and the farmer said—

"Thank you, my little lass, for mending my stockings so nicely, they are as strong as when they first came from the shop."

Lily blushed and said she was very glad he was satisfied with them, she had done her best, and should be so pleased to do anything more.

He looked at her good-humouredly, and said—

"Lass, I should like you to live at my farm-house, with my wife and family. What say you to this?"

"That I should be delighted to go and live with you," answered Lily quickly.

"What! leave all your kind friends here?"

"I shall be very pleased to go with you," again answered Lily.

"Then, lass, the missus says you may go. I shall leave this afternoon at about 5 o'clock, it is now 12, so lose no time in packing up your clothes, that you may be ready to start with me."

Lily left the room quickly. Her heart bounded with delight at the idea of leaving a place where she had suffered so much, although there was a mixture of pain in the thought that she should probably never again see good Mr. Heslope, but yet she felt that even on his account it was better for her to leave, and thus save him the constant trouble he had about her in his family.

"There," said Mrs. Heslope in a triumphant tone, "you see, Mr. Brandon, I was right. There is not a spark of gratitude or love in that girl. She has been with us nearly four years, and yet she accepted your offer at once to go and live with you, a stranger, without a word of regret at leaving those who have given her a home for so many years; I could cry when I think of such ingratitude," and Mrs. Heslope took the corner of her white apron, and feigned to wipe her eyes, and then blew her nose vigorously.

"Well," responded Mr. Brandon curtly, "the lass looks to me so sad, so frightened, and so crushed, that she scarce dares say her soul is her own. If you really have been as kind to her as you say, her appearance and looks belie you terribly. No slave with a taskmaster's whip held over him could look more cowed than that poor lass does, when you or your daughter speak to her. I hope she will look rather different when she has been in my house six months, and have a little more colour in her cheeks."

Fresh Sorrows Arise. 129

Lily at this instant entered the room, and heard the last kind words of Mr. Brandon. She looked at him gratefully, but did not dare say a word, so he took her hand, gave it a jolly shake, and said—

"Cheer up, lass, we will try to put a little more flesh on your poor bones, and make you look like a rosy apple, not an old white turnip."

Lily smiled and blushed so deeply that the farmer said, laughing—

"Didn't I tell you, lass, that I should bring colour into your cheeks, and it is beginning to come already. Now run and pack up whatever you have, then come and have a bit of dinner with me, and we will be off."

And Lily did run to pack up her clothes with a lighter heart than she had had for years. She wrote a few lines to say good-bye to Mr. Heslope, to thank him for all his kindness, and to say that she accepted the offer of the farmer to enter his service, because she felt he could not afford to keep her any longer. She gave this letter to Mrs. Heslope, and begged her to give it to her husband when he returned home. She then took some refreshment with Mr. Brandon, after which he harnessed his horse, got into his dog-cart, put

Lily into a warm corner with her small bundle, and drove off.

Lily took a last look at the place where she had suffered so much, thanked God for removing her, and begged His blessing on the new life which was before her. By degrees her feeling of shyness went off, for the farmer talked to her most kindly, and questioned her as to what she had done during her four years' residence at Mr. Heslope's. She told him all she had suffered, and likewise all she remembered about her own dear father and mother.

The burly farmer was almost moved to tears at the touching account, and answered—

"Well, my lass, you will have nothing to suffer from unkindness in my house, but I fear that in the out-of-the-way part of the country in which I live, you will have little chance of finding your father. However, you can try it for a bit."

CHAPTER XI.

LIFE OF LILY AT THE FARMHOUSE.

FARMER BRANDON'S horse was a good one; it trotted on briskly, but the distance they had to traverse was great, the roads were heavy and hilly, and he often stopped for a couple of hours to let the horse rest, and have some hay and water. Consequently they did not reach the end of their journey before the evening of the second day; then they drove up to a large, old-fashioned, strongly built farmhouse, which was the property of Farmer Brandon.

It was a picturesque building, with a thatched roof and curiously-shaped windows with small diamond-shaped panes of glass. The honeysuckle round the porch, and the ivy intermingled with roses, sweet-scented clematis and jasmine which mantled over a large portion of the house, gave it a cheerful and rural appearance. Lily was charmed, she had never seen anything like it before, and her exclamations of delight pleased the farmer.

They stopped at the door, and the carriage was soon surrounded by his family, who were anxious to greet him on his return home.

Mrs. Brandon came first, and he gave her a good hearty kiss on each of her plump red cheeks, and all the rest of the family followed; all were delighted to see him again, but the first question was—

"Who is this girl whom you have brought with you?"

"Well, my dears, she's a lass whom I thought might be of some use to my missus, for she can stitch anything; she mended such a big hole in my stocking. The folks she was with were sick and tired of her, and didn't care who took her, so as they got shot of her. I thought we might give her a trial as she was willing to come with me; she seemed frightened out of her life of the folks she was with, and longing to leave them."

"Well, I don't know that she'll be of much use to us," answered Mrs. Brandon, "for the girls could mend your stockings and do that sort of thing if they liked."

"If they liked, missus, yes,—but as they never do like, my stockings remain in holes."

Lily looked with pleasure at the broad good-humoured face of the farmer's wife, and was amused at the unmistakable likeness between the parents and the children. There were three boys and three girls, varying in age from ten to twenty. All were short, rather fat, rosy, and square in their proportions. They all stared at Lily, but as they looked at her with a good-natured expression, she was not much alarmed.

Mrs. Brandon then said—

"Well, my good girl, I must look out for a bed for you somewhere, but where I do not exactly know. Should you mind sleeping in the loft (where there is a small room) on the clean straw, if I gave you a couple of good blankets and a pillow?"

"Oh no, ma'am, I can sleep anywhere."

Mrs. Brandon went to the door, and shouted out—

"I say, Tom, shake up a good bundle of clean straw in the little room in the loft, and then come to me for some blankets to carry up there."

Tom soon appeared; he was a pale, gawky-looking chap, who did not seem to know exactly what to do with his long arms and legs. He was a good lad in many ways, but having been much cowed by his parents in childhood, was an awful coward, and would, I am sorry to say, tell a lie without hesitation to save himself a beating or even a scolding.

Lily was so tired out with the long jolting journey, that after taking a slight meal she begged to be allowed to go to bed, and as both the straw and the blankets were quite clean, she was very comfortable, and soon fell asleep.

She awoke next day quite refreshed. She could hardly understand where she was, and for a few moments fancied that she had been awakened by the dreaded sound of Mrs. Heslope's cracked bell. The events of the last two days, however, soon flashed on her mind, and she laughed at finding that the sound which had roused her was only the tinkling of the bells on the necks of some of the cows, which they wore to facilitate finding them if they strayed away on the neighbouring mountain. However, she got up quickly, dressed, and went downstairs to ask what she could do to be of use. They asked her to wash a few dishes, and clean up some things before breakfast.

She did this gladly and cheerfully, and Mrs. Brandon praised her diligence, which was quite a new thing for the poor child who had been accustomed to nothing but rebuffs.

After breakfast the girls brought her a pile of stockings, all of which were worn into such large holes that she saw that to mend them would take a week, at least; but she did not mind, for Mrs. Brandon came into the room soon after, and quite laughed when she saw the great heap, and said—

"Oh, what lazy girls mine are; these stockings ought to have been mended a month ago. I am so glad you can do them, my dear, but you need not work too hard; when you are tired of stooping over them, run out a bit in the garden, or come and help me in the kitchen."

Lily's eyes filled with grateful tears at this unexpected kindness. She thanked Mrs. Brandon and said she was accustomed to sit and work for hours at a time, but that she was sure she should be able to get through a great deal more, if she had a rest between times either in the kitchen or in the garden.

She soon got acquainted with the whole family, and liked them all in different ways.

They were somewhat rough and countrified, it is true, but kind-hearted and open; they could not be much companions to her, for they were so unlike in every respect; she was naturally refined, and they were bluff, and at times almost vulgar.

In point of fact she made a companion of Tom more than of any one else, and she did this not exactly from any pleasure she found in talking to him, but from an idea that she might improve his character by instructing him a little, as he was totally ignorant on every point save milking the cows, feeding the pigs, and weeding the garden.

One day when he was cleaning the pigs, he chanced, by mistake, to tread on a young pig which was only a day old, and killed it. Lily saw him do it, and was very grieved, as she was sure he would get a beating, as he so often injured things from carelessness. She quite trembled when the farmer came up to look at his pigs. He immediately saw the dead one, and asked Tom what had happened to it. To her surprise he replied—

"'Spose the old sow killed he."

"Dear me," said the farmer, "that is unfortunate, she is usually such a careful mother. I am afraid she had too many; but did you see her kill it?"

"She sitted on he, and crushed he flat."

"It doesn't look very flat, Tom."

"Look at the head of he, maister, the eyes be crushed out."

"So they are, Tom; well, it's very unfortunate, but cannot be helped."

The farmer walked away, and Lily instantly went up to Tom, and said—

"O Tom! how could you tell such a lie? God will certainly punish you some day."

"Never seed He, miss. Don't know if He hits hard; but I knows well enough that maister hits hard, and I doesn't like to feel his stick."

"Oh, but, Tom, you'll never go to heaven if you tell lies."

"Where's heaven, miss?"

"Oh! up in the skies, and when you get there you'll be so happy; no sticks or beating there, the angels fly about and sing all day and all night."

"Then I shouldn't like to go there, miss, for I can't abear music and singing; when Miss Susan sings and thumps that pianny, I always stop my ears and run out of the room."

"Oh! but Miss Susan screams so! The angels sing so soft and sweet, and so beautifully; and you'll sing too, Tom."

" Na, miss, na. I be's sartain sure that if I began to shout, they'd soon call out, 'Hold your jaw!' and to hear them angels go on sing, sing, sing, all day and all night too, would soon send me mad, in no time at all."

"Oh no, Tom, you'd like it very much, I assure you, indeed you would."

" I'll tell 'e what, miss, unless you've been to heaven and seen it yourself, I doesn't believe a jot about it; those things are said to amuse folks. I remember all the tales that were told about 'Meriky—that the trees were so big that a hundred men could stand in a hollow one; that there were such lots of gold in some parts that the chairs and tables were made of it; but when Bill O'Flannagan went out, he said none of that was true, that he never see a gold chair or table, and never could get any gold at all—that all the accounts were humbug! So I never believes anything unless I see's it. I'd believe if you had see'd it, miss, because you be's so awful petticular about what you call a lie."

" Ah, Tom, you'll find some day that there is

a heaven, and a hell too, where the devil will punish you, if you go on telling lies."

"Hope not, miss; I think I could wallop a devil any day, for I'm awful strong, but I daresay there is no devil at all either."

As Tom said this he walked away laughing. Lily felt very sorry for him, and half provoked; but he looked so good-natured and merry that she could not help laughing herself at his funny ideas, and she could not be angry with him, but determined to try and teach him to know better.

Lily's life at the farm was quiet and monotonous, but Mrs. Brandon and the girls taught her to make butter and bake bread. All three were fat and lazy, and delighted to get any one to do their work; they did not take much notice of Lily, but yet were never unkind.

Mrs. Brandon was one of those active persons who are always on the go, bustling to and fro from the dawn of day until quite late at night, therefore she had but little time to speak to Lily; and the farmer and his sons were in the field all day, so that, in fact, she could not help feeling at times a little lonely; and the remembrance of her dear mother and father sometimes filled her mind so completely that she could think of nothing else, and her longing to find her father increased, and she prayed even more fervently that she might one day have that happiness.

She thought, too, of Phœbe, her good kind friend, and wrote to her when she first came to the farmhouse, but as the letter was returned, concluded she had left when her mother died, and therefore it was useless to write any more.

She could not at times prevent a feeling of anxiety and sorrow, when she reflected on the isolated position of the farmhouse, and how impossible it was for her father to hear anything about her in such a wild and unfrequented part of North Wales, and there was no one to whom she could speak of her feelings. Mrs. Brandon would have exclaimed (as she did once when Lily ventured to express her longing desire to find her father)—" Law! bless the child! what do you mean? What can you care for a father who must have quite forgotten you by this time? What can you want more, child, than you have here? plenty of victuals to eat, and as much drink as you like (which is not much to be sure), and a good warm frock too, and a clean bed, and not over much work."

Lily replied by thanking Mrs. Brandon for her kindness in every respect, and never again mentioned the subject of her wish to find her father, but she continued, nevertheless, to offer up her constant and fervent prayer.

She had one friend in the farmyard who soon loved her devotedly, and this friend was a large black mastiff called "Lion." All the family liked it more or less, therefore it was better off than most dogs; but every dog that is tied up suffers at times, even when it is what is called properly looked after. It must be repugnant to the nature of any animal to be unable to move but within the length of a short chain, and the delight evinced by a dog when let loose proves it beyond all dispute; but that is not so bad as what frequently happens, the being left for a day or more without water, not from any intentional neglect, but from the carelessness of those who have charge of the dog; then again, in the summer the kennel is frequently so placed as to render it impossible for them to find any shade. Servants will pass a dog a thousand times, and perhaps give it a kick for whining, without ever looking for the cause of its complaint. If it is sitting outside its kennel panting in the sun, they will only say—

"Of course the dog likes the sun, or it would go inside its kennel." They never reflect that the kennel, from standing all day with the hot sun pouring down upon it, is even worse in point of heat than the outside.

Lily had naturally a feeling heart, and seeing the dog one day panting in the hot sun tried to send it into its kennel, and when it refused to obey, put her own hand in to feel if it was nice and cool; she was astonished at the heat, and understood at once the reason why the poor animal would not enter. She ran to Farmer Brandon, and asked his leave to put the dog in a cool place. He answered with a hearty laugh—

"Please ye'self, lass, only mind you tether it up safe, for it's a savage beast and would bite any one. I wonder you are not afraid of it."

"Thank you," said Lily, "I'm not in the least afraid of Lion."

She then went to look for Tom, and told him that his master had given leave for the dog to be moved out of the sun. This was soon accomplished, and Lily was quite rewarded for her trouble by the happy and grateful look of the poor beast as it stretched itself out comfortably in the shady corner selected.

On another occasion she was passing through the yard and saw Tom, who was usually so good-natured, give the dog a great kick, saying in a surly tone—

"Larn better manners, sir, and stop that howling; you kept me awake half the night."

"O Tom! why are you kicking that poor dog? See how pitiful it looks."

"He must be punished, miss, to larn he to be quiet. Didn't 'e hear the shindy he kicked up last night?"

"Yes, Tom, I heard the poor fellow moaning so, that I was very near getting up to see the cause. What could have made it whine so?"

"There was a cat about, and maybe a rat too, that he wanted to be after."

"No, Tom, no; it did not sound a bit like that. Did you feed it yesterday?"

"Oh yes; and I gave him a jolly lot too."

"But has it any water?"

"Always has plenty, miss."

Lily went up to the bucket and looked in;

not a drop of water was there, and the bucket was nasty and dirty as if it had been used for other purposes.

"See, Tom, the poor dog has not a drop of water, that was the cause of the howling in the night."

"Dang it, and you're right," said Tom. "Bill Champ must have used it yesterday morning to empty the pig bucket, and he's such a careless chap that he never thought of cleaning or filling it again."

"And so the poor dog has been left since yesterday morning without water, and beaten for whining to ask for some."

"Yes, miss; but I'll fetch some now."

Tom ran across the yard and soon returned with a bucket of nice clean water, which Lion commenced drinking with the greatest avidity, and when its thirst was satiated lay down quietly in the kennel, not forgetting, however, to wag its tail almost off in thanks for the relief Lily had procured. She re-entered the house feeling quite pleased at having saved the poor animal further suffering, and this did not happen once only but very often, sometimes in one way and sometimes in another; consequently the dog became excessively fond of her, and would obey her instantly.

To the cat, likewise, she was a kind friend. It belonged to the girls, who were supposed to feed it regularly, but they often forgot it. If Lily heard the creature mewing before bed-time, she would creep downstairs when all were asleep, and give it some milk, particularly if it had kittens. She said nothing on the subject to any one, lest she should offend the girls; but she could not sleep if she knew it to be suffering.

She was generally industriously employed in mending and making the greatest part of the dresses of the family, and she likewise helped a little in cleaning and dusting the house, and was always ready for any odd job, such as gathering fruit for preserving, making hay, or even weeding in the garden, and when all was finished she had a little leisure time, which she employed in reading some books she found in an old cupboard.

These books were supposed to have been left there by a young lady who came to the farm for change of air, and died of consumption in the course of a few months. Her relations carried away all her apparel and other goods, but left these books as useless lumber; and useless lumber they were as far as the Brandon family were concerned, for they never troubled themselves even to open them, but to Lily they were invaluable treasures, she read them over and over again. They were all instructive, mostly history or travels, but likewise there were a few spiritual works, in which she delighted. Many happy half-hours did she spend in perusing these books, and her mind and intellect expanded rapidly.

The quiet life, fine country air, and good food soon caused Lily to look very different from when she left Mr. Heslope's. She grew in height, she was no longer thin, although still very slight, and she had some colour in her cheeks. There was a natural refinement in her manners and appearance, which made every one in the farmhouse consider her as above themselves. Tom always called her "miss," as he said she looked so much more like a lady than either Miss Betty, or Miss Sally, or Miss Sukey, and no one seemed to think it strange for him to do so. Altogether, her life was a peaceful and happy one.

The farmhouse was unfortunately at a great distance from any church. She could never

Life of Lily at the Farmhouse.   147

get there more than once in the month, as the cart in which they went only held four persons; but she tried to be content with what Providence had ordained, and determined to remain quietly where she was, unless anything happened to show that a change would make things better, and that the farmer and his wife approved of her leaving.

A year passed by, two years passed, a third was almost completed, and Lily was still living quietly at the farm, when one morning an unusual event occurred. The postman brought a letter, and this letter was for Mrs. Brandon. She opened her eyes when the postman delivered it to her, for as she could not write, no one ever thought of addressing a letter to her, more especially as she could not read writing. But there was no doubt that this letter was for her, and the postman left it, laughing heartily at her surprise. She soon opened it, but then the question was, who was to read it? She could not, nor could her husband; each son and daughter tried in turn, but all in vain; they could not make any sense out of it, they spelt out a few words, but that did little good.

At last the farmer thought of Lily. She was

called, and asked if she could read writing. She took the letter, and got through it without much difficulty,—she would have had no difficulty at all, had it not been very badly written and very badly spelt.

This letter was from a cousin of Mrs. Brandon to say that a friend of hers, one of the first milliners in London, wished for change of air before the commencement of the season, and being rich, would pay handsomely for a comfortable apartment at any farmhouse in a healthy situation in North Wales.

The cousin had immediately thought of Mr. Brandon's farm, as she felt sure they would give up one of their best front rooms on the consideration of being well paid for it, and of course the two elder girls could attend on Madame Rosa, the lady in question, and Mrs. Brandon, who was a tolerable cook, would be quite equal to satisfying her in that line.

This letter caused quite a commotion in the farmhouse. The girls were pleased, as they thought this fine lady would know all the fashions, and show them things they had not seen before. Mrs. Brandon was pleased, as she thought this new acquaintance might be an advantage to her daughters. Farmer Brandon too was pleased, because he calculated that this visit would be an advantage to his purse which happened to be rather empty at that time.

So they asked Lily to answer the letter, and say that the room would be ready for Madame Rosa any day she liked to name in the following week. Lily immediately wrote the letter required as nicely as she could, so nicely, indeed, that Farmer Brandon was delighted, and declared that Lily was the best lass that had ever entered his doors, and that she must be the attendant on the fine lady, as she looked a vast lot more genteel than his girls.

The girls both tossed their heads a little when he said this, but as they were really good tempered they did not mind much, therefore Lily did as she was desired, and began at once to prepare the room for Madame Rosa. She arranged what furniture there was as nicely as possible, put some vases for flowers on the chimney-piece, and made a little dressing-table of an old deal box she found in the hay-loft. Mrs. Brandon gave her a white cloth, and some old muslin which she washed, ironed, and arranged so as to make the table look quite pretty. The girls wondered at her thinking of such a thing, but she did not tell them that she arranged this pretty dressing-table from what she remembered in her dear mother's room. She could not tell them, lest they should laugh, as every remembrance connected with that dear lost one was sacred to her.

She then put white muslin curtains to the window, which improved the appearance of the whole. The floor was as clean as possible, and when Mrs. Brandon had put down a bit of carpet by the bedside and before the dressing-table, the room looked as nice as any one could desire.

It was agreed that Lily was to call Madame Rosa in the morning, and take her a jug of hot water. She was to take her some at night, and be ready at any time in the day to attend on her.

On the appointed day Madame Rosa arrived, and Mrs. Brandon met her at the door with smiles, and many excuses for the deficiencies of a farmhouse, which must cause some annoyance to a lady like her.

Madame Rosa was not prepossessing in appearance; she looked proud and stuck-up, and made very little answer to Mrs. Brandon's polite speeches; she merely said—

"I came down here for country air, and did not expect anything particularly comfortable; but I am tired with my journey over your horrid roads, so show me my room, whatever it is."

Mrs. Brandon was rather taken aback by the proud manner of the London lady, and complained to her husband; he, however, only laughed and said—

"Never mind, missus! never mind, she'll pay us well, and a few pounds are better worth having than a thousand smiles and pretty speeches. I've been counting up what her rent will mount to in three weeks, and I find I shall be able to purchase the cow I was wishing for."

The only person in the house whom Madame Rosa noticed much was Lily. She seemed quite to like her gentle attendant, and asked her to do many extra things in the way of mending and making things she required during her stay; she even condescended to teach Lily to make a pretty cap which she gave to Mrs. Brandon, and to trim three hats, one for each of the girls, and one for Lily herself.

These little presents pleased Mrs. Brandon

and the girls so much, that they quite forgot how much they disliked the proud, off-hand manners of Madame Rosa, and declared she was a charming person. Neither of the girls, however, looked half as pretty in their smart hats as Lily did in the simple one which Madame Rosa selected for her.

One day Madame Rosa asked Mrs. Brandon a few questions concerning Lily, as she was puzzled to imagine how such a pretty, lady-like looking young girl could have come to be a servant in an out-of-the-way farmhouse like that, among such a rough countrified set.

Mrs. Brandon told Madame Rosa all she knew of the early life of Lily, and how when she first came to them from Mr. Heslope's she looked so thin and pale that you could almost see through her, but that she had gained strength and health wonderfully since that time.

Madame Rosa seemed greatly interested, and afterwards talked to Lily herself on the subject.

"You cannot suppose," she said, "that you have the slightest chance of finding your father in this out-of-the-way part of the world?"

"I fear not, indeed," answered Lily sadly; "it is that thought alone which makes me not as happy and contented here as I ought to be, considering all the kindness that is shown to me. But what can I do, madame? I have no friends in the world, I cannot go anywhere else."

"In London you would have more chance of hearing something, especially if you were in a fashionable part of it—that part, for instance, in which my establishment is situated. You seem to have a taste for millinery; what say you to going to London with me and joining the young ladies of my establishment? You would, at different times, see every grand person in London, and you might hear things that would lead to the discovery of your father."

The eyes of Lily sparkled with delight at the idea of such a happiness, and she answered quickly—

"Oh! how very kind of you, madame, to propose this. I do really think it might enable me to find my dear father, but I will not think of any change without first consulting Mr. and Mrs. Brandon. They have been so kind to me that I would not do the slightest thing without their sanction and approval."

"Very well," answered Madame Rosa, "talk

to them about it, for I am quite willing to take you and have you taught the business."

Now, all this sounded very kind in Madame Rosa, and so thought Lily; but, in reality, there was not a spark of kindness in her intentions, for she was a vain, selfish woman, and thought of nothing but what would answer her own ends. Lily was pretty, genteel looking, and handy at dressmaking, therefore she thought such a girl would in time form a valuable addition to her establishment, and consequently was anxious for the proposal to be accepted. She cared not whether the poor girl discovered her father or not, but she cared a great deal for anything that might draw fresh customers. She was a person who would make use of Lily while she suited her purpose, and then fling her away like a faded flower when no longer useful.

Lily went at once to Farmer and Mrs. Brandon to tell them all about Madame Rosa's proposition, and to ask them whether they thought she ought to accept it and go with her to London, in the hope that in such a fashionable part she might hear something to lead to the discovery of her father.

In her heart she almost hoped that the farmer would advise her not to go, as she looked upon Madame Rosa with a feeling of fear, and doubted whether she could be happy with her; besides which, the family of the farmer had been very kind to her, and she loved them all gratefully. The hope of finding her father was the only thing which tempted her at all.

Farmer and Mrs. Brandon listened attentively to all that Lily said, and the former then replied that he could not give an opinion at once, but would talk the matter over with his Missus.

He did so, and likewise spoke to Madame Rosa on the subject, to ascertain exactly what her intention really was, and whether her business was sufficiently good and lucrative to give Lily a fair start in life.

Madame Rosa said that she was willing to take Lily as she was nice-looking, and handy with her needle, but that, with regard to future prospects, her success would depend in a great measure on herself. If she was active and clever in the business she would be sure to get on, and that, of course, in such a large and fashionable establishment, in the best situation in London, she would have more chance of finding her father than she could have at a farmhouse in such an out-of-the-way part of Wales.

Farmer Brandon then called Lily, and said—

"I have reflected well on the matter, lass, and have likewise spoken to Madame Rosa, and I am come to the conclusion that, although I am mortal sorry to part with you, yet that it is better for you to accept her offer. You will, of course, have far more chance of finding your father than you could ever have here, and I fancy you will be able to earn a good livelihood as a milliner and support yourself respectably, in case you never find your family. And I must likewise tell you another thing, my lass, which is, that I am thinking of emigrating to Canada with my family before the end of another year. I do not wish it spoken of as yet, but my mind is quite made up. You know my eldest son is married and established there; he wishes me to join him, and I think it is the best thing I can do, as trade is bad, and the cattle disease, which has ruined so many, has likewise much decreased my live stock. Therefore, all these reasons put together make

Life of Lily at the Farmhouse. 157

me advise you to accept the good lady's offer, and I wish you both happiness and success in your new life, and I am very sure that we shall all miss you much."

Lily thanked the good farmer with tears, not only for his advice, but likewise for the constant kindness he had shown her. She felt the idea of leaving them all immensely, more especially as she knew it would be quite useless to attempt to write, as they could not read her letters, nor could she receive an answer, as not one out of the whole set could write a readable letter.

Poor Tom was in despair when he heard that Lily was going to leave, and live with the fine London lady, for in his rough way he was very fond of her, thought a good deal of the advice she had given him, and had profited by it on many points.

"Well, miss," he said one day, "I do really think I will try to go to heaven, as I should like to have a sight of you again, and I am sartain sure that, if there is such a place in the skies for good people to go to, you will be there."

"No, Tom, you must try to be good to please God."

"But you told me I must try to be good that I may go to heaven and see God, so if I like better to be good to go there to see you, what difference can it make to He? none at all, for He'll see me there all the same, and I needn't say why I came, need I, miss?"

Lily could not help laughing, and scarcely knew what to answer, but said—

"Well, all you have to do to get to heaven is to try and be good; and if you get to heaven and I get there too we shall be quite happy; and when you see God you are certain to love Him, because He is so beautiful and good and kind; so now, mind, Tom, you tell no more lies, and say your night and morning prayers carefully."

"Yes, miss, to please you."

"No, Tom, to please God."

"Well, I'll try to please God, to please you, but I wish you were not going away, for I do love you so; and when you are gone, too, no one will mend my stockings, or put a button on my shirt."

"Tom, I am very, very sorry to leave you all, but I am going to London in hopes of finding my father."

"I hope you will find he, miss; and won't he be pleased to see you again, grown so nice and tall and rosy."

Madame Rosa announced her intention of returning to London in a week, and desired Lily to spend that time in putting her small wardrobe in order, as she would have little time for her own needlework when she commenced life as a milliner.

Every one in the farmhouse regretted the departure of Lily. The three girls, because she was so obliging and saved them so many scoldings for their idleness. The farmer regretted that dear, cheerful, little lass, who had a kind word and look for every one. Mrs. Brandon regretted her, too, gave her many kind words of advice, and arranged numerous comfortable articles of dress for her use.

At last the morning of departure came, and Lily could not help crying very bitterly when the carriage came to the door, and when she raised her head and looked round she saw that every one else was crying too.

Tom was sobbing outside the door, and stuffing his great dirty fists into his eyes to stop the tears, but the only effect the fists produced, was making the tears, as they ran down his cheeks, look like very dirty muddy ditch water, and as he did not possess a handkerchief, his face had completely the appearance of a greasy bit of bacon just taken out of the pot. So wet and untempting did his face look that, although Lily kissed every one else, she could not make up her mind to kiss him, which he, poor lad, seemed quite to expect, but she contented herself with giving his hot sponge-like hand an affectionate shake, saying—

"Good-bye, Tom, do not forget your promises, but keep them faithfully."

"Yes, yes, miss," sobbed poor Tom; "I'll do my best, no one can do more, can they?"

Madame Rosa was in the carriage, so Lily had to get in without more delay. They drove off, and were soon miles away from the farmhouse. Lily continued to weep bitterly for some time, but Madame Rosa paid no attention to her tears beyond saying once—

"La! child, what a figure you are making of yourself,—how silly you are to cry so for nothing."

CHAPTER XII.

THE MILLINER.

WHEN Madame Rosa arrived at her house in London, she sent for her forewoman, Miss Carson. This lady soon made her appearance, and obsequiously expressed the delight she felt at the safe return of the mistress of the establishment.

Madame Rosa responded curtly, pointed at Lily, who was standing trembling at some distance, and said—

"I hope you will make this young person useful in the establishment; her appearance is in her favour, and she can assist you in the show-room. Of course she will be shy and awkward at first, but that will mend by degrees."

Miss Carson looked at poor timid Lily somewhat scornfully at the beginning of Madame Rosa's address; but she brightened up at the last words, and said she would do her best—her very best—to make the girl of use in the establishment; but that some were so very awkward, stupid, and idle, that it was impossible to teach them much; however, she would do her utmost, yes indeed quite her utmost.

Miss Carson was a spinster of a certain standing, whose age was a mystery not easily solved. She insinuated and brought up chance circumstantial evidence to infer that she was scarcely thirty; her friends said that they did not think she was forty, but those persons (and they were many) who disliked her, asserted roundly that she would never see fifty again.

She was skilfully got up was Miss Carson; her morning toilette was no small affair, it usually occupied some hours. First, a mysterious mixture was applied to her hair to give it a bright tint, and hide the streaks of grey which continued to increase as time went on. Then she carefully pencilled both eyebrows and eyelashes, to make them dark, so as to give expression to her countenance and make up for the deficiencies of nature in that respect. After performing this little operation in the most artistic manner, her teeth had to be attended to; that is to say, false ones inserted here and there. She fancied, poor foolish old soul, that every one believed these teeth to be her own; and it is possible that some persons might have been deceived in this respect, had she been cunning enough to have had them less white and even. She might then have spared herself the trouble of constantly bringing up how "dear papa" had not lost a tooth when he died.

When the mouth furniture was complete, she scattered some white powder skilfully over the whole surface of her face, which was succeeded by pink powder on the cheeks.

In the beginning the rouge was applied lightly and artistically, but as years went on, the eyes of good Miss Carson became more dim, and unknown to herself the quantity of pink powder gradually increased, which her friends could not fail to observe, and many were the malicious speeches made on the subject.

Miss Carson remarked with dismay and trouble the gradual increase of wrinkles on her face; what could be done? She consulted an artiste in that line, who recommended a species of claw under the hair, which drew the skin of the cheeks tightly up, and thus lessened the wrinkles. Uncomfortable enough these claws were, in truth, but it mattered not, for "pride feels no pain," and these claws decidedly made her countenance more juvenile. In order to render her step light and elastic, she had small springs inserted in both boots, which so completely answered their purpose, that a person walking behind would be tempted to exclaim—

"How lightly that young girl trips on, she seems scarcely to touch the ground."

But if, alas! she chanced to turn round and show her made-up old face, the beholder could scarce restrain a laugh at his mistake; one young man, in fact, exclaimed quite in her hearing—

"Good gracious! I thought she was a young girl! and she is only an old hag!"

Miss Carson endeavoured to persuade herself that the words were said in reference to some other person passing at the time, but for all that she was careful in future never to raise her white gauze veil, hoping thus to disguise the ravages of time.

Miss Carson was the forewoman in Madame Rosa's establishment; she had been in this capacity for many years, and therefore had much influence. The young women, by whom she was viewed with awe and fear, flattered and made up to her; they soon perceived that the weak point in her character was the fear of being considered old, and although they despised her in their hearts, for this silly weakness, yet they pretended to believe that she was young,—young like themselves! They often expressed their admiration of the soft hair and brilliant complexion on which she prided herself; and she, silly old soul, believed their flattering speeches, revelled in the admiration she fancied she excited, and continued to paint and patch and talk nonsense.

But to return to Lily. Miss Carson desired her to follow quickly, and on entering the workroom instantly commenced questioning her, with the greatest curiosity, as to who she was, where she came from, and what friends she had; the timid young girl could not, of course, satisfy her curiosity on most of these points.

"I suppose you will like to go to the showroom," said Miss Carson spitefully, "as your appearance is in your favour?"

"What is the showroom, madam?"

"Oh, you stupid! why, the place where the ladies come to look at the smart dresses and bonnets, of course."

"If you please, madam," said Lily beseechingly, "do not make me go with you there, I should be so frightened. I have never seen a grand lady; I should only be in the way; do let me stay and work quietly here, I will do anything you wish me to do." Miss Carson looked more propitious.

"Well, you are right, child, you would look so stupid, and get laughed at by the fine folks, so you shall stay here. I will tell Madame Rosa how shy you are, and that you beg not to go into the showroom for the present. You really are quite nice looking, my dear; your eyes are like mine, blue, and your hair is quite as soft, and your mouth is shaped nearly like mine, only not quite so small. I shall pass you off as my sister, and love you with all my heart, my dear."

Miss Carson at these words kissed Lily, and caressed her with wonderful warmth. Lily looked up in surprise at this sudden burst of affection, and almost smiled at the idea of being sister to that quaint old spinster; had she said daughter or granddaughter, she would not have marvelled; but her depressed feelings prevented any burst of merriment, and as she was silent, Miss Carson thought she quite agreed in opinion, and introduced her to several of the young women belonging to the establishment.

They stared the poor girl almost out of countenance, and whispered remarks on her appearance to one another. Lily slunk into a corner to endeavour to escape further notice, but Miss Carson patted her on the back in a patronising manner, and said—

" Do you not perceive, young ladies, the great resemblance there is between this young person and myself? she has my eyes, my mouth, and my hair!"

" Yes, she is rather like you," exclaimed all the girls; "but she will never have your graceful manner, and her hair is not half as long or bright as yours."

" Perhaps not, perhaps not," responded Miss Carson triumphantly, " but then this poor girl has not enjoyed the advantages I have. I quite love her, dear young thing, and I shall do all in my power to promote her real interest, and teach her how to behave," said Miss Carson, bending over poor Lily, who was at a loss what to do, or what to answer.

The young ladies made signs of derision and began to titter, but restrained themselves, and were quite grave and composed when Miss Carson looked round before leaving the room. When the door was closed, and she was quite gone, their mirth burst forth, and they exclaimed with one voice—

"Oh! that silly old woman, who thinks herself a girl, and believes that we are taken in by her painted face and made-up appearance; an old goose! an old goose!"

Lily looked at them with astonishment, she could not understand such duplicity; bashful as she was she ventured to say—

"I think she seems a very kind lady."

Her words were received with a burst of derision—

"Oh yes! oh yes! very kind, very kind indeed! You will see after a bit how very good she is, Miss Innocent, wait a bit before you give your opinion."

Lily ventured not another word, but one of the young ladies, Miss Budge, who was good-natured, seeing her evident distress and how she trembled, went up to her and said—

"Never mind, my dear, we are having a little fun, but you will find out after a bit that Miss Carson is only kind to those who co not clash with her in the least. I mean to those of whom she is not jealous; if she once has cause to be jealous of you, all her love will vanish at once, and she will hate you and spite you as much as possible."

"But how could she be jealous of me, a poor friendless girl? it seems impossible."

"Ah! you will find that out in time; now be cheerful, it will be time enough to grieve when troubles come; but if Miss Carson proves a real friend to you, we shall all be surprised."

Lily determined to do all in her power to please Miss Carson, as also Madame Rosa; the latter she scarcely ever saw, but she soon became quite the right hand of the former, who kept her constantly employed, and even condescended to give her instructions in the art of dressmaking.

Miss Carson being, however, very selfish, consulted her own convenience in what she did for Lily. She took advantage of the anxiety of the girl to please, and made use of her, in return for every trifling lesson; she made her sit in her room and get through work entrusted to herself by Madame Rosa, and then went out to amuse herself for the evening.

The good girl did anything she was asked,

but found the life of a London dressmaker a weary, dreary one, and soon lost the little colour that was in her cheeks when she first arrived from the country.

The room in which they sat was small and close, and the hours of work were often extended far into the night. It was indeed most fatiguing to continue work, work, work, for so many hours, and the worst of it was, that when at last they were allowed to retire to seek the rest they so greatly needed, poor Lily was usually so overtired, so feverish, as to be totally unable to sleep. She often lay awake for hours, longing for a breath of fresh air, and then again and again thinking of her dear dead mother, of her lost father, and imploring God to grant her the happiness of seeing him once more, at least, before she died; for young as she was, there was a secret conviction in her heart that she should not live long. There was a feeling of weakness which was not natural at her age; and the unhealthy life of a dressmaker, the foul air she breathed, the hurried meals, the many hours devoted to work increased her debility. It often happened that when a fête was given by some great person, that such numbers of dresses were ordered at the same time, to be finished without fail before the day, that the poor young girls in the millinery establishment were almost worked to death. They were obliged to rise and commence their labours at a very early hour of the morning, and to continue working, almost without intermission, until a very late hour at night. Madame Rosa sent them strong coffee in the evening to keep them awake, and it had the effect of preventing drowsiness, but did not rest their aching heads and worn-out fingers; and when at length the weary task was accomplished, most of the poor girls were completely exhausted, far too exhausted to sleep. If the gay ladies for whom the beautiful robes were destined, had known of the sinking hearts, the aching eyes, and the worn-out fingers that had been employed over these dresses, their kind hearts (for many of these ladies had kind hearts) would have sickened at the thought of the suffering they had occasioned by the short time allowed for the making of these dresses; they could not have enjoyed a pleasure purchased by the sacrifice of the health and comfort of their needy fellow-creatures.

Could some of these favourites of fortune have

cast a glance at the pale, the wan, and extenuated countenance of Lily, as she sank down on her miserable and narrow bed, without sufficient strength and energy even to remove her garments, at the late hour of three in the morning, they would have felt tempted to throw their beautiful dresses into the fire rather than wear them—for the remembrance of her suffering countenance must have haunted them, and embittered all enjoyment; even the exhilarating music and the festive dance would have failed to restore their spirits.

The season, however, was drawing to a close, the work began to lessen, and the workwomen were no longer compelled to labour over hours, but during the time of bustle, even Miss Carson had been obliged to work very hard, and from not being young felt the fatigue even more than the juvenile members of the house; in fact, she was after a time completely knocked up, but yet would not own it, for fear of being desired by Madame Rosa to give up her place in the showroom to some younger person. She liked being in the showroom, as it gave her an opportunity of seeing every one who came, and showing off her airs and graces.

One morning, however, Miss Carson was so ill, and so weak, that she was utterly unable to leave her room, therefore Madame Rosa sent word that Lily was to attend in the showroom in her place, as she expected many customers to call on that morning to try on some bonnets and caps that were just arrived from Paris.

Lily was terribly alarmed at hearing what she was expected to do. She entreated Miss Carson to persuade Madame Rosa to let Miss Budge or Miss Prim attend in her place. But Miss Carson was really ill, and not having been able to perform her usual morning toilette, would not allow any one to enter her room, but called out in a sharp, querulous tone—

"Do as you are bid, child; go to the showroom, but take care not to talk too much, lest the ladies should think you bold; if you do, you'll have the worst of it, I can tell you, from Madame."

Miss Carson did not, I am sorry to say, give this advice from a kind motive. She knew well enough that Lily was far too timid to speak much, but she was anxious to make her shy and awkward, lest Madame Rosa should insist on frequently making use of the pretty modest young girl in her place.

Lily went immediately to the showroom where Madame Rosa was already seated.

"Take these bonnets out of the boxes, arrange them on this table, and place them so as to contrast the colours well."

Lily obeyed, and having naturally a good eye for colours, succeeded in satisfying her mistress, who then ordered her to put out the headdresses. After doing this, she retired to the farther end of the room, and sat down, and worked diligently until persons began to flock in to inspect the Parisian fashions.

First a bedizened old dowager sailed into the room, and insisted on trying on every bonnet and cap. Lily stood quietly and obeyed each order given.

"I am certain, dear madam," said Madame Rosa deferentially, "that this plum-coloured chapeau was made for you. It just suits your complexion; it contrasts so well with your fair skin."

"Yes, it suits me pretty well; but that pink one, with white flowers, would be far more becoming. Here, child," turning to Lily, "put it on me. Law! child, how stupid you are, and your hands are so cold, do stand farther away!"

This exclamation was not caused by any stupidity on the part of Lily, but the old dowager was irritated when she saw the face of Lily reflected in the glass before which she was trying on the bonnet, for the contrast of the pretty fair countenance of the young girl by her side, made her own face look even more worn and ugly than when seen alone; she almost dashed the bonnet she was trying on to the ground, and shoved Lily on one side, exclaiming—

"I do not like any of your bonnets or headdresses, Madame Rosa; there is a far better assortment at Marshall & Snelgrove's; I shall go there at once."

She marched out of the room indignantly as she said these words, and Madame Rosa, who was much put out, scolded Lily for being so awkward, said she had disgusted one of her best customers, and bade her be more careful in future.

Madame Rosa spoke thus to Lily because she was out of temper herself, and was glad to vent her spleen on some one, and in truth she did not perceive the real cause of the anger of the dowager.

The next person who visited the showroom was a spinster of forty years standing. She tried on every bonnet and cap, praised them all, and ended by taking nothing, to the infinite disgust of the mistress of the establishment.

A mother and her two daughters came next; the object of their visit was to order a bridal dress for the youngest of the two.

"What should you recommend?" said the mother, addressing Madame Rosa.

"I should decidedly recommend a rich white satin, with a Brussels lace flounce, and trimmed with white Parisian flowers. I have a beautiful assortment, if you will please to look at them."

"Yes, yes, but be quick, for we have so many other places to go to this morning; my daughter is to be married, as you know, at the end of this month."

"I have heard so, my lady. Lily, bring the large square box which stands in the shop below, on the right hand side as you enter."

Lily instantly obeyed, and when she had left the room the young ladies whispered to one another—

"What a pretty girl that is! Did you ever see such beautiful eyes, and she looks so gentle too, so unlike a shop-girl, but sadly delicate and fragile."

When the flowers were brought they were duly examined by the mother and her daughters, and Madame Rosa was pretty well satisfied, as they purchased a large quantity, and promised to return the next day to select the satin and lace for the bridal dress.

Other customers came in; some looked at everything, gave no end of trouble, and bought nothing, others purchased a few things. Lily found it most fatiguing to wait on them; they never gave a thought as to whether she was tired or not, they seemed to look upon her in the light of a machine, only put in the room for them to use and work as long as they pleased.

At last, to the immense relief of poor Lily, the hour arrived for closing the showroom, but she was obliged to put every bonnet and cap up in its place, as they had been left here and there by the thoughtless ladies; this took her a full hour, as Madame Rosa sat and directed everything; then, and not until then, was she allowed to return to the workroom.

She went immediately to see Miss Carson, who this time admitted her into her bedroom, as she was anxious to hear how the afternoon had passed off. She questioned Lily very closely as to the number of ladies who had called, what they said, what they purchased, and how she liked attending on them.

Lily blushed, and said she was afraid she had done very badly, that she was certain she had offended one old lady very much, although she could not understand how, and she was so tired, too, oh! so tired; she hoped Miss Carson would be well enough to take her own place next day, and let her remain in the workroom as usual.

Miss Carson looked very pleased, and replied graciously—

"Of course, my dear, you could not be expected to understand, as I do, how to behave and give satisfaction to ladies. I have been accustomed to the first society for so many years. But I shall be quite well to-morrow, as I am much better this afternoon, and I shall be able to take my own place again in the showroom."

Lily then returned to the workroom, where she was assailed on all sides by questions from the young women, who were curious to hear every possible particular about the ladies she had served, who they were, what they had purchased, and what else they were likely to order. The bridal party, in particular, interested them immensely; they endeavoured to make out who the bride was, and who she was going to marry.

Lily was, however, unable to satisfy their curiosity, as she was unacquainted with the names of any of the customers, but she described the future bride as tall, elegant in appearance, with bright golden hair, and skin like alabaster. Both sisters had gentle countenances, and seemed very kind. Of the mother she had felt a little afraid at first, as her manners were slightly abrupt, but she even was good at heart, for she said to her—

"You must be very tired, my child, with standing the whole afternoon, for you do not look overstrong."

None of the other ladies had thought in the least whether she was tired or not.

The next day Miss Carson announced herself quite well, and ready to attend the company in the showroom. She went there in capital spirits, proud to feel that those who had called on the previous day, would be struck with the difference between her graceful manners and Lily's shyness and awkwardness.

Some ladies from the city came first. They looked at many things, and Miss Carson's obsequious manners pleased them, but for all that they purchased little, and endeavoured to beat down the price of everything. Next came the bridal party, and this time accompanied by their brother, a dashing-looking youth. Miss Carson approached, and asked them in a deferential tone what she might have the pleasure of showing them.

To her great disgust, however, they made no reply, but said to Madame Rosa—

"Where is that pretty girl who waited on us yesterday? We quite fell in love with her, and my brother came with us to-day on purpose to have a peep at her."

"She does not usually attend the show-room," said Madame Rosa; "she is very shy."

"Oh! never mind that," answered the bride; "she is too pretty to be shut up. Send for her at once, or I shall go somewhere else. And let me give you a few words of advice, Madame

Rosa," she continued, casting a smile of contempt on poor, discomfited Miss Carson, "if you wish your bonnets and head-dresses to sell well, keep that young girl in your showroom, and let her put on the bonnets and hats to show them to advantage. Persons will expect to look as fascinating in them as she would. Where did you meet with such a pretty creature?"

"I fell in with her quite by chance," responded Madame Rosa. "If you really do wish it, I will send for her at once."

"Of course we do," said the ladies in a breath.

Madame Rosa turned to Miss Carson, whose lowering countenance showed the anger in her heart, although she could not change colour, for the simple reason that painted faces cannot alter their hue, and are therefore no index of the mind in that respect.

"Go at once and call Miss Lily to attend on these ladies, and I see no necessity for you to return at all."

Miss Carson stood as one transfixed, and did not reply for a moment, but Madame Rosa exclaimed in an impatient tone—

"Dear me, how deaf you are, Miss Carson! do make haste and call Miss Lily at once."

Miss Carson walked slowly towards the door. She did not attempt to trip lightly, no, her heart was too heavy,—heavy with anger, with jealousy, and hatred for the poor girl who thus, unknown to herself, had supplanted her, had robbed her of the much-loved office of attending the showroom. Her anger was not mollified by hearing a burst of laughter as she closed the door, and the words—

"What an absurd old woman that is! She makes herself look a hundred, by her funny juvenile dress, and all her paint and false hair."

Poor Miss Carson! She could not make up her mind to tell Lily to go to the showroom, so she gave the message to one of the young ladies to deliver. The young lady hastened to call Lily, and said laughingly when she found her—

"Good luck for you, Madame Rosa desires you to go to the showroom, and if I can judge by Miss Carson's angry face you are to go there in her place; and if so, you will soon discover why we called you Miss Innocent for thinking her kind."

Poor Lily did not comprehend the meaning of these words, but replied—

"I am afraid poor Miss Carson must be ill again, I am so sorry; but could not some one else go to the showroom instead of me, I got on so badly yesterday—I was so frightened!"

"No, it is you whom Madame Rosa has sent for, so you must lose no time in going there, or she will be precious angry, I can tell you."

Lily obeyed instantly, and on entering the room felt pleased at seeing the ladies who had spoken kindly to her the day before, but the sight of the gay brother made her wish to run out again, her poor pale face became almost crimson. She was, however, quickly roused by the sharp voice of Madame Rosa, who said—

"Come in at once, do not stand at the door blushing and looking so silly."

Lily advanced slowly and timidly.

"By jove you are right," whispered the young man; "she has the finest eyes in all London, and she casts them down to show her fine eyelashes. She knows what she's about; she's a brick, and no mistake."

"For shame, Archibald," said the mother; "do you not see that you are frightening the poor timid girl so much, that she does not know where to hide herself?"

Lily fetched a hat indicated by Madame Rosa, and attempted to put it on the head of the bride; but in her fright she put it on with the front behind, which caused bursts of laughter among the light-hearted happy young people, and Lily felt ready to sink into the ground when Madame Rosa pointed out her mistake in an impatient tone.

The mother, however, put her hand gently on the poor girl's shoulder, and said with a smile—

"Never mind, my dear, you can soon put it right again, you are a little shy, that is all." And turning to her son she whispered, " If you continue to stare, and make remarks about the poor girl, I will go away at once."

The young man looked quite ashamed, twiddled his moustache, took up his hat and stick, and marched out of the room without another word. Lily then did her utmost to give satisfaction to the ladies, and succeeded so well that Madame Rosa was quite pleased, and told her that she would be of great use in the establishment in a short time, if she took pains, which Lily promised to do.

Numbers of other persons came that afternoon, and Madame Rosa sold a great deal, which put her in high good humour, and she praised Lily so much that the poor child left the room with a more happy heart than she had had for years.

She went quickly to look for Miss Carson, thinking that she would be pleased to hear all the events of the day, and how much better she had succeeded than on the previous afternoon; but she was not in her usual little room, so she went to the workroom, hoping to find her there and quite well. There she was, in truth, but not working. She was seated in a low chair, her hair, usually so smooth and glossy, was rough and tangled, and fell in untidy masses over her face. Three or four false tresses had fallen from her head and were lying on the floor at some distance, but she did not remark it, although at any other time such a thing would have filled her with dismay; no, she did not move, but sat, still, prim, and stiff, apparently unconscious of what was passing around her. Lily was quite alarmed when she saw her, approached quickly, and exclaimed—

"Oh! my dear Miss Carson, what is the matter? Are you ill? Is there anything I can do for you?"

Miss Carson made no reply, but cast a contemptuous glance at Lily, muttering some incoherent words, and at the same time motioning her to depart at once.

Lily looked up in astonishment, and said—

"I only came to tell you all that took place this afternoon in the showroom. I thought it would amuse you; I thought, too, that you would be glad to hear how much better I got on to-day in attending the ladies, and that Madame Rosa was quite pleased with me."

Miss Carson remained stiffly seated in her chair, and would deign no answer save—

"Be off, old bold face, be off!"

Lily listened in astonishment, totally unable to understand how these words could refer to her; but as Miss Carson would not even look at her she turned away sorrowfully, and she was leaving the room when she heard her exclaim, between hysterical sobs, to Miss Budge, who was near—

"Oh, my dear, what would you have said if you had seen her conduct in the showroom? it made me almost die of shame, and a young officer who came there with his mother was so disgusted that he took up his hat and left the room—I heard him swearing all the way downstairs!"

Lily did not remain to ask a question, but left the room, for a glimmering of the truth dawned upon her mind. She could not but remember the kind words of the ladies, and how grieved she herself was at Miss Carson being told not to remain. Innocent as she was, the case was too apparent; she felt that Miss Carson was jealous of her. Miss Budge happened to pass at the moment, and Lily entreated her to tell her what she had unknowingly done to offend the forewoman. Miss Budge smiled maliciously and answered—

"Some persons are very kind when they have no reason to be jealous! Remember what I told you the very first evening, Miss Innocent!"

Lily turned first red and then pale at these words; she felt, alas! that they were true. She entered her room, sat down, and wept silently. There was no sullenness, no anger in her tears. She called to mind the advice given her on so many occasions by Phœbe, and she placed her sorrows where every good Christian should place them, and found the peace she sought.

CHAPTER XIII.

SAD CATASTROPHE CAUSED BY JEALOUSY—TAKES REFUGE WITH AN OLD APPLE-WOMAN.

THE evening of that unpleasant afternoon passed over drearily, but on the following morning Lily arose from her broken slumbers comparatively calm. She hoped that during the night Miss Carson would have reflected on the injustice of her conduct, and that matters would go on quietly as usual; she determined to do her utmost to avoid going to the showroom.

But vain, alas! were her hopes. There was no change for the better in Miss Carson, she maintained a dignified silence, and rarely spoke excepting to find fault with Lily. The young ladies, one and all, thought it incumbent on them to follow her example; therefore the position of poor Lily was rendered so wretched that she quite rejoiced when the afternoon came, and she was ordered by Madame Rosa down to the showroom.

About two months after these painful events she was sent out one afternoon by her mistress, with a bandbox containing a very rich dress—which she was to take to the house of an old lady who lived at no great distance from London Bridge—to be tried on.

The dress when tried on was found to require much alteration, therefore Lily was obliged to carry it home again.

She was crossing London Bridge, and met a poor old man, who stopped her to beg relief. She had only a penny, and the purse containing it was in her pocket; therefore she rested the box, in which she had placed the costly dress, on the parapet of the bridge, and put her hand in the pocket of her dress in order to get out this purse, at the same time asking the poor old man a few questions about his sick wife, whom she chanced to know. Suddenly, however, a menacing voice sounded in her ear, uttering reproaches, and accusing her of losing time gossiping on the bridge.

She looked up hurriedly and saw the spiteful, angry face of Miss Carson, who was standing behind and shaking her fist at her. This sight caused such a start that she ceased for a moment holding the bandbox with her left hand, it fell, and notwithstanding all efforts made to catch it, tumbled over the parapet into the rapid river below; and in a few seconds she saw it whirling round and round in an eddy,—and then it was quite lost to sight.

Lily stood, perfectly transfixed with terror, even Miss Carson looked a little alarmed, as she had not calculated on such a result; but she soon recovered, laughed in a spiteful manner, and said with a satanic grin—

"This comes from gossiping when sent out on an errand! I'll tell Madame Rosa all about it, that you may depend on." And she trudged off without another word.

Lily remained motionless, white as a marble statue; she neither moved to the right or to the left, she knew not what to do; she did not dare return home, but where could she go; who would give shelter and protection to a poor friendless girl. It was November, the afternoon cold and foggy, and the dim daylight fast disappearing. She felt sadly alarmed at the thought of remaining alone in the street at that hour, but what could she do ? it was impossible to return home, impossible to brave the anger of her mistress; for she felt certain that the jealous, the spiteful Miss Carson would tell every one that she had dropped the dress over the bridge from carelessness, that she had been gossiping with the old man to whom she had just given the penny. The experience of the last few months had convinced Lily, beyond doubt, of the hatred of Miss Carson, whose only wish now seemed to be to get her expelled from the establishment; and she was fully aware, moreover, that the spite and malice of the irascible forewoman would prevent any scruples as to truth, if it could forward her evil design; therefore she decided in her own mind, that even death from cold and exposure in the streets would be preferable to returning home without the dress.

Suddenly she heard a voice addressing her; she fancied it was that of Miss Carson which resounded in her ears; she started with terror, sprang forward like a frightened fawn, and ran without looking behind to ascertain whether the fear was groundless or not. This time terror gave her wings instead of paralysing her;

she hurried down the bridge almost with the swiftness of an arrow from a bow, and was soon at a great distance from the scene of her disaster.

The voice she had heard was not, however, the voice of Miss Carson, but that of the poor old man to whom she had given the penny. He had seen all that had taken place, and guessing her position from the words of the angry forewoman, he had raised his voice to address her and endeavour to persuade her to return with him to his poor dwelling and sick wife, as there she would, at least, have shelter and some protection from the inclemency of the weather.

The state of panic into which she was thrown had, however, prevented her from recognising his voice, and the louder he spoke the faster she ran. It was, of course, vain for a poor, feeble old man to think of pursuing a young, frightened girl. He walked a short distance, but soon stopped, judging the case hopeless, and fearing a crowd might collect, as a number of idle boys were on the alert, anxious for a lark, and ready to get up a cry of "Stop, thief!" He turned back and wended his steps towards his home, uttering a prayer as he walked on that God would move some one to show that mercy to the good young girl that she had shown him, and which had caused her so much suffering.

Lily ran on, fancying Miss Carson was in pursuit. Fatigue compelled her, after a time, to slacken her pace, and she was filled with even greater dismay on perceiving that she was in a part of London which was quite unknown to her,—all around seemed strange. The streets were narrow and dirty, there were no shops, merely a few fruit and vegetable stalls here and there.

A man was just lighting the lamps, but they were so few and far between, that the lurid glare they shed in their immediate vicinity served to make the long intervals between them still more dark and gloomy. It rained a little, and the atmosphere below was so cold that the drops froze as they fell; the streets were thick with dirty London mud, and there were no boys employed in sweeping the crossings. It seemed as if the neighbourhood was so poor that no one would give a penny to a sweeper, therefore it was left unswept.

Lily's shoes were quite wet, but in crossing

a very muddy part of the street one of them stuck so fast in the mud that she could not draw it out. At that moment a butcher's cart came down the street, driven at a furious pace, and she was forced to jump hurriedly on one side, leaving her shoe in the deep mud. When the cart was passed and she returned to hunt for it, she could find no shoe; it was buried in the mud which the cart and horse had dashed through, and the night was too dark to see anything, so she was obliged to walk on with only one shoe.

She came to an old archway and determined to take refuge there, crouching down in a corner behind a large rough stone which had fallen from the side. She hoped to spend her night there unperceived by any one, but a policeman soon passed through with a lantern in his hands, and saw her. He instantly gave her a rough push, and said—

"Pass on, girl! no tramps are allowed to remain here; pass on, girl!"

She obeyed, arose at once, left the poor shelter of the archway, and again walked on, looking in vain for some place in which to spend her dismal night.

She tried to rest for a few moments by leaning on some iron railings, opposite a large building, but she was quickly told to "move on," or she should be sent to the House of Correction for the night. The idea of such a disgrace was dreadful to her, so she moved on quickly. Had it not been for the disgrace, she would have been thankful for a night's lodging anywhere.

Suddenly she was accosted by a young woman, who told her, in a soft voice, to come along, and she would give her a night's lodging, and a good supper into the bargain. Lily started and looked up, anxious to express her gratitude for the proffered kindness; but when she saw the bold countenance, the painted, bedizened form, and the malicious leer of the person who addressed her, she shrunk and shook with a greater fear than she had felt at the rough words of the policeman, and again took to her heels, and ran so fast that, although the young woman followed, she was unable to catch her.

She ran on from street to street, fancying the woman was still in pursuit. She ran, until at length she stopped at the corner of a back street where she saw the stall of an old Irish apple-woman, who had not yet returned to her lodging for the night. She entered the stall with clasped hands, and tears running down her cheeks, and implored the old apple-woman, for the love of God, to allow her to remain for the night.

The old woman had a benevolent heart. She was much moved by the evident distress of the poor young creature, and immediately answered with a smile—

"Yes, sure, my honey, come in, and welcome. But what makes you out alone so late at night, in this bitter weather too? Have you lost your way? or have you no home?"

The kind face and motherly tone of the old apple-woman encouraged poor Lily. She told her all the particulars of her cause for distress and fear, the jealousy of the forewoman, the severity of her mistress, and the utter impossibility of returning home without the expensive dress which Miss Carson had caused her to let fall over the bridge into the river.

"Oh! if you would only allow me to remain with you, I should be so happy. I would help you in your apple stall; I would do anything you wished that was not displeasing in the sight of God. Oh, do let me remain with you!" said Lily in a beseeching voice.

The good old woman reflected, and said—

"I am very poor myself. I have great difficulty in earning sufficient to keep body and soul together; how can I undertake to keep another? You would not probably procure me more customers than I have now. I fear that I cannot prudently venture to take you, my dear child."

Lily did not reply, but stood with clasped hands and an imploring countenance, looking at the old woman, and inwardly praying God to move her heart.

Biddy M'Graph (for that was the old woman's name) continued to reflect. She was a good and fervent Catholic, and her only wish in life was to please God. Could she refuse to take charge of the poor, motherless, friendless, dejected creature who now implored her help, and whom He had perhaps guided to her stall? Could she hope for mercy if she now refused mercy? Oh no! she will receive the poor child from His hand, and trust to Him for the means of supporting her.

So she turned to the anxious girl and said to her gently—

"I will not turn you adrift, my honey, you shall remain with me until you like to make a change. You may find the life you will lead with me too hard, for you look a frail weak crathur, but I will do my best for you, colleen."

Thus was the prayer of the good old man on the bridge granted, Lily received from Biddy that mercy which she had shown him. It would be difficult to describe the feeling of gratitude and happiness which overflowed the heart of poor Lily, when she heard the decision of old Biddy; but her words were few, for she was so completely exhausted by walking for so many hours, by want of food, and misery of mind, that she could scarcely stand. The kindly woman soon perceived this, and pulled out from the bottom of a huge pocket a small bit of bread and meat which some young persons, who were just returned from a picnic to an old abbey, had given her out of the basket which was so nicely filled with every delicacy, in the way of food, when they left London in the morning for their day's pleasure. What they gave her chanced to be a remnant of chicken sandwich, and Lily, who could not in her very weak state have touched anything coarse, ate it with grateful eagerness, and was much refreshed. The old woman then told her that it was quite time to close the stall, as there would certainly be no more customers that night, and they must walk to her lodging, but before starting she looked by chance at Lily's feet, and perceived that she had only one shoe.

"Och, my child, and how comes this?" she exclaimed; "you cannot walk with only one shoe. What have you done with the other?"

Lily told Biddy how she had lost her shoe in the mud, and was unable to find it afterwards in the dark.

"Well, my purty colleen, that was sad, but what can we do now? It is half a mile to the house where I lodge, you cannot possibly walk that distance, on such a night, without a shoe. Let me see, I must try and find something to give you in its place."

She hunted through a quantity of rubbish that she kept in the old deal box she sat upon, and at last exclaimed in a triumphant tone—

"Here it is, this is just the thing for you." She held up an old worsted slipper. "This belonged to my dear old man, who died ten years ago, come next Christmas."

Lily took it with thanks, but it was large enough to contain at least four feet the size of her foot.

"'Tis a trifle too long," said Biddy, "but we can stuff in some paper to make it smaller; it will then fit quite nate and aisy."

The paper was inserted, but the slipper was still so much too large that it dropped off directly she tried to walk. Biddy then endeavoured to tie it on with a bit of string which she found in the box, but all was vain, it was useless to think of wearing the huge slipper. At last Biddy dived again to the bottom of the old box, and brought up a small parcel containing a nice-looking pair of boots, which she kissed and wept over to the astonishment of Lily.

"Who do these boots belong to, mother?" she said; "they would just fit me, I think."

"Then take 'em, my child, and wear 'em."

"But who do they belong to?" Biddy did not answer. "Do not tell me if it pains you," said Lily gently, perceiving that tears were running down the cheeks of the old woman; "put them back in the box."

"No, no, my honey, keep them, wear 'em and

welcome. They belonged to my poor boy Tim ; oh ! such a good lad was my Tim, the pride of my heart !—and he loved his poor mother too."

" But where is he ? is he dead ? "

"Oh yes, my honey, my poor boy is dead long since."

"Was he ill long, mother ? "

"Oh no! he was strong and blythe as could be when he left me, and half an hour after they carried him home on a shutter dying."

" Had he met with an accident, mother ? "

"Yes, yes, my child. He was walking fast to do an errand for me, and he passed close to a ladder under a scaffolding. The workmen had carelessly left a hod of bricks and mortar on the scaffolding at the top of the ladder when they went to their dinner, and just as my boy was passing a gust of wind unsteadied the ladder. It fell on one side, and in doing so caused the mortar and bricks to fall, and one large brick fell upon my Tim and knocked him down flat on the pavement. He was soon picked up, but he could not either stand or move, his back was hurt (so the doctors said). They carried him home, but he couldn't speak a word even to his poor mother. He looked up and down so strange, and he groaned—oh! I can hear his groans now, the darlint,—but I sat by him and watched him, and I wouldn't give up my place to any one save the praist, who soon came. He looked at my dear boy and said, 'Alas! it is all over with him.' And so it was; I knew it, I felt it, but I sat by his bed and never ceased looking at him. All at once his poor pale face turned red, and then almost black, he opened his eyes wide, looked at me, and said, 'Mother!'

"I started up, I put my face close to his dear face, but I could hear nothing more. I looked again and again, and I listened, oh! how I listened, but he was gone—gone from his mother. I longed, oh! how I longed, to hear him say 'Mother' once more, but he never moved or even groaned again. And the next day they put my Tim into his coffin, and we had a wake, and he was buried, and I have lived alone ever since; and I kept his shoes and looked at them each day, and tried to fancy I should see the dear lad come in to put them on, looking blythe and gay as he always did. But you shall have them, my darlint, and welcome; you shall not be without a shoe to your foot."

"No, no, indeed, my good, kind Biddy; I will not take what you value so much."

"And sure, but you shall. And maybe God has sent you to me that I may take you to my heart and love you as I did my Tim, so put 'em on at once, colleen, and may the blessing of God be upon you. And now we will start at once."

They started. The night was still dark and cold, the streets narrow and muddy, but Lily's heart was light, so she tripped on briskly. She felt that she was at last in the hands of a good and religious woman. She thanked God for His mercy in directing her steps to the fruit-stall, and notwithstanding the fatigue she felt, insisted on saving her feeble friend the trouble of carrying the heavy basket of apples. The weight was, however, rather beyond her strength, and she was not sorry when a boy, whom they met driving home in his donkey-cart, stopped them and said—

"And sure, granny, that basket is far too heavy for you and that 'ere young 'un to carry. I've just sold all my load of vegetables to Paddy White at the corner of the market, so I'll put yer basket of apples in my empty cart.

I'm going yer ways, and I'll set it down at yer door. Ye desarves a good turn for sitting up so many nights with my old mother. I shan't forget that in a hurry, as sure as my 'dad's' name was Pat."

He laughed good-humouredly, took the heavy basket without an effort, put it in his cart, gave his donkey a poke, and jogged off.

Lily tripped on by the side of her friend, not sorry to have got rid of the heavy basket. They passed through numbers of narrow, dismal-looking streets, and met (to her surprise as it was so late) many respectable looking persons, who were just going out as if on urgent business.

Most of these persons, although poorly clad, had the manners and appearance of ladies; many of them stopped to say "good evening" to Biddy, and to ask if they could do any commission to save her from the necessity of going out again that evening. She thanked them gratefully, but said she wanted nothing.

Lily asked Biddy who these persons were, and was told in answer that most of them had seen better days; some had been governesses, others shopkeepers; but not having saved anything were reduced in their old age, *when* past work, to the greatest poverty, and lived in the most miserable lodgings. They never appeared during the day, for fear of meeting persons who had known them when well off, but they went out in the evening to make their purchases for the following day.

"How is it that they are so poor?" said Lily; "I thought governesses were paid so much better than servants. I always wished to be a governess, that I might have something to give to others, and be able to save myself from going to the workhouse, when I am old and not able to work."

"I bean't able to tell you much about that," said Biddy, "but you will soon get acquainted with those who live in our court, you can ask them, and they will soon explain everything. There is one who lives only two doors from us; she is ill, and very bad off, but oh! so good, so patient, so kind, and so clever too. She's got lots of big books, and I do believe she knows everything that's in 'em. When she first came here she had an old mother to take care of, who lived with her, but she's dead now, and she ives all alone. I look in at her most days, and take her a sup of tea when she's poorly, which is pretty often, and now you'll be able to do that for me, colleen. I shall make you over to her, you'll love her so."

"No, indeed, mother, you promised to let me live with you; I will not leave you for any one."

"And you shall not leave me, my poor darlint; but there's many the time when you'll like some better one to be with than old Biddy. When I reach home, and have had my supper, I takes me pipe by the fire, and sure and sartain I falls to sleep pretty soon, and then I'm but poor company. Now, you're young, and won't need a pipe and backy, but you'll want some one to cheer you up in the long winter evenings, and then, darlint, you'll go to her, and hear her talk, and see her pictures and books and work."

"What is her name, Biddy?"

"Her name is Miss Sinclair."

"That is a pretty name. I hope she will like me, but I am afraid of strangers."

"Oh! you'll not be afraid of her, depend upon it."

"Is she tall?"

"No, not very tall; but so thin, so very thin,

that you fancy you could see through her. She had a terrible cough a short time ago, but it is better now."

" Is she handsome ? "

" No, not handsome, her face is too pale and thin. I daresay she was well looking a few years ago, for her eyes are black, and shine brightly at times; but the pretty part of her face is her smile, it lights up her face, and looks like a gleam of sunshine when the sun comes out suddenly on a foggy day. But you shall see her this evening, my child; you shall go with me after supper and take her a nice apple which we will roast at our fire, she can eat that sometimes when she can touch nothing else."

They walked on, and after a time arrived at Biddy's lodgings, which consisted of only two rooms and a small back-yard. A neighbour had lighted the fire, and the water in the kettle was singing and ready to boil, therefore the good old woman was able to make a warm cup of tea for the cold shivering girl, which revived her wonderfully.

There was little enough of furniture in the room, and nothing but a bit of matting on the floor opposite the fireplace; but all looked as clean as anything can look in dirty smoky London, and you could see that the floor was often washed. There was only one chair and a stool in the room, but Biddy made Lily sit and rest on the chair, whilst she bustled about the small room making preparations for supper. Then she went into the other room to see what could be arranged in the way of a bed for Lily; and after some consideration came to the conclusion that for the present it would be best for Lily to share her bed, for the scanty stock of bedding divided would be quite insufficient; and both would be frozen during the night for want of covering. Lily was willing for anything, and the good old woman was most anxious to make her as comfortable as her slender means would allow.

After their frugal supper they talked over things a little, and agreed that Lily should stop at the stall and sell the fruit when Biddy was required to remain at home to wash and cook, but that when Biddy had nothing to do at home, Lily could take a basket and sell watercress.

"You will find it a hard life, I fear, my honey," said the kind old woman; "but God will take care of you, and you will be more happy, I feel sure, than you've been for many a long day; and I will take you to his Reverence —good Father O'Hara, who will give you comfort and advice whenever you need it; I have known him all my life."

CHAPTER XIV.

A KIND FRIEND.

"And now, my honey," said Biddy, "you must come with me to see Miss Sinclair; I fear she is not well, as we did not meet her this evening; we will take her this baked apple."

Lily followed Biddy to the door of Miss Sinclair's lodgings. They raised an old broken latch and entered a dark, dismal, damp room, tenanted by a surly old woman, who continued smoking a broken pipe, and did not utter a word when they entered. Biddy, however, said kindly—

"Is Miss Sinclair upstairs?"

"'Spose so," was the surly answer, and puff, puff went the smoke from her pipe. So they crossed the room, went through a species of outhouse, and commenced mounting the miserable broken staircase which led to Miss Sinclair's room.

There was no light, so they had to grope their way up as best they could; and they must have fallen, without the assistance of a rope which was fastened to the wall. Biddy knocked at the door, and a low, but sweet-toned voice responded, "Come in."

They entered the room, which was small and low; it was not papered, but whitewashed, which gave it a tidy appearance. The low bed was in a corner, and a curtain hung before it and the wash-hand stand; so that the room looked like a small parlour. A few good prints, mostly on sacred subjects, were plainly framed and hanging on the wall. A deal table stood in the middle of the room, but it was covered with a neatly embroidered cloth. The window curtains were of netted thread, tastefully lined with an inexpensive pink chintz.

There was only one window in the room, but this was rendered cheerful by a few pots of bright flowers, which had been brought to her from the country by a young girl whom she had taught to read and write. These plants were evidently tended with the greatest care, and they looked green, and clean, notwithstanding the smoke and close air of London.

Opposite the window, and close to the wall, stood a small chest of drawers ; and on it a painted bookcase filled with the large and small books which Biddy had described in such glowing colours to Lily.

Everything in the room was neat, and the manner in which all was arranged showed, beyond mistake, that the inmate of this room was a lady—a lady who had seen better days, and had brought some remnants of former tastes to decorate her present poor and humble abode.

Biddy presented the baked apple to Miss Sinclair, who was seated by the small fire and reading. She took it with thanks. A grateful smile lighted up her delicate countenance, and gave it that appearance of sunshine of which Biddy had spoken, but she seemed very weak and unwell. Perceiving Lily, who stood behind Biddy, she said—

"You have a companion to-night; may I ask who your young friend is?"

Biddy told Miss Sinclair a few particulars about Lily, to which she listened with both interest and pity ; she took her hand, pressed it gently, and said—

"Be comforted, my poor child, you have indeed suffered much, but you will now be safe from harm, and will meet with every possible kindness from my good old friend here; and I hope you will come and see me often, and I will do anything in my power to endeavour to help you, and make you happy. Are you fond of reading?"

"Indeed I am, madam," answered Lily, looking with eager delight at the books on the shelves, which seemed to her an immense library. "I have had very few as yet, for indeed I have always had so much work to do, but if you will lend me a book sometimes to read in the evening, it will be such a pleasure to me; and I will be most careful not to soil or injure it."

"Indeed I will, my child, you shall have any you please. My books are mostly instructive, but I will explain anything in them that you do not understand. Come to me in the evening, when Mrs. M'Graph can spare you, and you shall read some of the books with me, and I will teach you all I can; for when your father returns, my child, he will be delighted to find that you are not uneducated or ignorant, and I feel sure that he will return and find you at last."

Lily gazed at Miss Sinclair with grateful delight, and could hardly find words to express her thanks. She listened with admiration to her gentle voice and lady-like expressions. She contrasted in her own mind the quiet self-possessed manner of Miss Sinclair, with the fussy obsequious flattering manner adopted by Miss Carson when she wished to render herself agreeable, and wondered at the immense difference. She felt sure that she should love Miss Sinclair, and shuddered when she thought of Miss Carson. But Biddy told her it was time to return home, so they wished Miss Sinclair good-night, and re-entered their own lodging.

After warming themselves for a short time Biddy said to Lily—

"And now, me darlint, we will kneel down and ask God's pardon for the faults of the day, beg His blessing on the future, and thank Him for the blessings we have received."

Poor Lily slept little that night, but her heart was tranquil and happy; she was not in the least alarmed at the prospect of the somewhat hard life she was to lead, every bitter was sweetened by the thought of the kindness of her new friends, and the comfort of being near a church and good priest to whom she could apply for advice and help if needed. At Madame Rosa's she never had a half hour in the day to spare, and she was constantly obliged to work the whole of the Sunday, more especially during the London season, when the ladies required their dresses to be finished and brought home in time for some grand ball. She had pined and longed for religious comforts, and sometimes endeavoured, when alone with Miss Carson, to get her to speak a little on such subjects, but her endeavours were vain—Miss Carson used to open her eyes wide and exclaim—

"Law! child! what do you mean? are you a Methodist? I thought you were only a Papist."

So poor Lily was quickly silenced, and had to content herself with thinking over the simple instructions given to her by Phœbe, and she likewise had the most vivid recollection of the saintly words and pious practices early instilled into her mind by the dear mother who had been so suddenly taken from her. She constantly implored our Lord to grant that she might discover her father, and implored His Mother to be a mother to her. She prayed with simple faith, and felt sure that God would grant her prayer some day.

Biddy rose early on the morning after the arrival of Lily. She got up noiselessly, not to disturb the placid slumber into which the poor girl had at length fallen, as she hoped that a few hours of extra sleep would restore her strength and spirits.

She lighted the fire in the little kitchen, made the kettle boil, and then placed it by the side of the fire that it might keep warm, ready for Lily to make a cup of tea on first coming downstairs. She herself took a few crusts of bread to soak in a drop of buttermilk which had been given to her the day before, and hurried off to the stall, to be ready for customers who usually paid her a visit and made some purchases on their way home from the eight o'clock service in the neighbouring church. Lily, as we said before, did not sleep much during the early part of the night; her agitation and state of excitement had been too great for her to calm down quickly, and when at last she did doze a little she was quickly wakened by the snoring of Biddy. At last, however, towards morning she dropped into a sound sleep, and did not even miss her companion, who got up, dressed, and went downstairs at five. When she awoke up the clock had struck nine, and it was some time before her thoughts were sufficiently collected to remember the events of the past day, or to understand why she was in a strange room, and a strange bed; by degrees, however, all flashed upon her mind. She jumped out of bed quickly, and thanked God most fervently for having directed her steps to the stall of good old Biddy M'Graph.

When dressed she went downstairs, and immediately remarked with grateful feelings the kind thought of Biddy in putting water in the kettle, and some tea in a cup on the table by the side of the teapot, that she might be able to make a cup directly she came down.

After her small breakfast she looked round the room to see what she could do to help Biddy. Had she known the way to the stall she would have joined her there, but she did not, as they came home in the dark. She, however, went upstairs, and found in an old drawer several pairs of worn-out stockings, which she immediately began to mend. The holes were so large that it seemed almost a hopeless task to make them even wearable, but she worked diligently, and by the time Biddy returned had made one pair look so tidy that the poor old woman was delighted, and said she had not had such a good stocking to her foot for many a long day, no, not since Peggy O'Shea died of cholera three years before.

Biddy brought home a bit of bacon to fry for their dinner, which they ate with some good potatoes roasted in a neighbour's oven. When their repast was finished, Biddy asked Lily if she would like to go with her to the stall that afternoon, as from its being market-day, she was certain of many customers, and her assistance would be very welcome. Lily was delighted at the idea of being useful, and they started at once.

"Now," said Biddy, "you must try, my honey, to remember the way we go, that you may be able to return home alone if you wish to do so. You may be quite tired out before I am ready to return home. First, we walk to the end of this long street, then we turn to the left by that baker's shop, then go on straight until we come to the third turning on the left, which is a very narrow street, and leads into a place called Lincoln's Inn Fields. Pass right through, and you will come to a street filled with shops and stalls, and at the end of all these you will see one standing almost alone, and that is mine."

Lily listened attentively to these instructions, and when they at last reached the place, told Biddy that she was certain she could find her way back to their lodging without difficulty.

They remained at the stall until past five, and had what Biddy called a good afternoon, for they sold almost the whole of her stock of apples. Some of her best customers were schoolboys, who passed through the street by chance, and seeing her fine rosy apples stopped to ask the price, and finding she was reasonable in her charges, filled their pockets with them. One little boy alone stood and looked with longing eyes at the beautiful apples and nuts, but when asked which he would take, answered with a sigh—

"I cannot buy any, I have not a penny in the whole world. I had a penny this morning, but little Minnie begged me to give it to her to buy a bun ; I could not refuse her, so now I have nothing left to spend."

Lily looked at Biddy beseechingly (as she longed to give the poor little boy the nice rosy apple he was looking at), and whispered—

"May I give it to him?"

"Yes, sure," answered Biddy, with a smile; "and a handful of these nuts to boot."

Lily instantly put the apple and the nuts into the hands of the small boy, who received them with surprise and delight, and was walking away from the stall with them, when a great tall bully of a boy came up suddenly and knocked both the apple and the nuts out of his hand, exclaiming at the same moment—

"You young thief! what business had you to prig that apple and those nuts? We all know quite well that you have not a penny to pay for them—you young thief! you young thief!"

The young urchin began to cry, and to explain that the apple and the nuts were given to him, but his words were received with jeers and contempt. Biddy tried to explain matters and exonerate the poor child from blame, but all in vain, no one listened, and each boy having purchased what he wished for turned away, leaving Charlie to blubber, as they termed it, and find his apple and his nuts as best he could. He tried to do so, but in vain; the street was a slope, and the apple ran on, bumping up and down faster and faster, until at last it was lost to sight at the bottom of a dark dirty gutter. Whilst he was pursuing his apple the street urchins picked up the nuts, and cracked and ate them before he could turn round.

Biddy would willingly have given him some more fruit, but he, perceiving suddenly that all his companions were gone, ran after them as fast as possible, and was soon quite out of sight.

"It is useless," said Biddy, "to try and give anything more to the poor child; so as it is now beginning to get late we will return home and have a bit of warm supper."

They started, and having sold all the contents of their basket, it was not very heavy to carry, but Biddy said her pocket was quite heavy with halfpence, therefore she stopped to make it lighter by purchasing a nice fat bit of pork at a large bacon shop they passed on the way home.

They quickly reached their dwelling, and Biddy soon cut up the pork and commenced frying it, whilst Lily made the tea. The cooking was soon accomplished, and both sat down to their repast with light hearts and excellent appetites. When Lily lived at Madame Rosa's she scarcely took enough to keep a sparrow, she could eat nothing at all. The close rooms, the want of fresh air and exercise (so necessary for the young), made her unusually weak and delicate, but now, from having been occupied the whole afternoon in the open air, she felt like a different creature, and enjoyed her slice of fried pork more than she had relished anything for months.

When all was finished, Biddy said—

"And now, colleen, I will take you to see Father O'Hara. He is certain to be at home, as he always remains in the church or in his house the greatest part of the evening, as most of his congregation are poor, and it is the only time they can come to him for advice or instruction. And after you have seen him you shall go and pay Miss Sinclair a bit of a visit, while I sit by the fire and smoke my pipe."

Lily was delighted at the proposal, and was

ready in a very few minutes to start for the house of the good priest. They found him at home as they expected, and he received them in a most kind and fatherly manner.

Biddy soon recounted every particular about Lily, and her many sorrows, to which he listened with the greatest interest; and he told Lily that she need never fear coming to him for advice if she required it, as he should always be delighted to help her in any difficulty. He kept his word, for although it was not in his power to bestow a large amount of time on each separate individual, on account of the size of his congregation, which was composed of the poorest of the poor, yet whenever she did come to him he never failed giving her some words of comfort and encouragement. When he got to know her better he was both pleased and astonished at her great innocence and purity of character, and he marvelled how one, who had been so much exposed in the world, could have preserved these qualities untainted.

CHAPTER XV.

MISS SINCLAIR EDUCATES LILY.

WHEN Biddy and Lily left the house of Father O'Hara, they went to Miss Sinclair's lodging and separated at the door, Biddy returning home, while Lily knocked at her new friend's door. It was quickly opened, and Miss Sinclair welcomed her with a smile and a kiss, which she returned with affectionate gratitude. They sat down and talked of many things, and Miss Sinclair pointed out to Lily the books she should advise her to read first.

"When you have read a little, my dear child, I shall recommend you each evening to write out what you can remember of what you have read, it will form your memory, your handwriting, and your style. This will be such an advantage to you in after life, when you are once more under your dear father's roof; think of his satisfaction at finding you all that he can desire, and worthy of being presented to his friends as his long lost and beloved daughter."

Miss Sinclair kept her word, and she took the greatest pains in teaching Lily, who, on her part, found no difficulty in learning anything. She had an excellent memory, and the greatest facility in understanding all that Miss Sinclair explained to her.

It was really astonishing to see how she remembered and wrote extracts from the books she had read. Having a sweet voice, and a correct ear for music, Miss Sinclair, who was herself an excellent musician, taught her many pretty. songs, and instructed her in the theory of music.

"Do you not think that I might be a governess like you in time?" said Lily, one day when Miss Sinclair praised the extracts from English history which she had just written. " I am sure it would be a far more happy life than that of a dressmaker, and I sometimes fear that I shall not be strong enough to stand in the apple-stall and brave the inclemency of the weather for many years."

"Oh no, dear child; never think of such a thing," answered Miss Sinclair quickly.

"Do you think I shall never be clever enough? I will take such pains, I will do everything I can to improve."

"It is not that, my child; you will soon know quite enough to teach young children, but you do not know—indeed, you do not know—what a life of trial, what a life of privation and suffering, is that of a governess. I perhaps suffered more than most, because I was not born or educated to gain my living."

"How, then, was it that you became a governess?" said Lily, looking earnestly at Miss Sinclair. "Do tell me a little about your former life. I have so often longed to ask you a few questions, but I never dared, lest you should think me curious."

Miss Sinclair patted Lily fondly on the head and said—

"I could never think you either rude or curious, my sweet child; but the history of my trials and sorrows is a painful one. I scarce trust myself even to think of it, and I have been so often recommended to endeavour to banish all thoughts connected with my early trials, that you must forgive me if I am silent now. Later I may be able to speak on the subject with

Miss Sinclair Educates Lily.

more calmness, and then I will promise to give you the history of my life. It may interest you, and you will, at least, see that trials are the portion of every one in this world. To some they come at one period of life, to others at another period, but come they will, whether we try to avoid them or not."

"Thank you," answered Lily quickly, "I am content to wait as long as you please, and I hope you will never tell me your history at all if it gives you pain to do so."

So no more was said about it at that time, and Miss Sinclair continued to instruct Lily on every subject calculated to be useful in her future life, as she had an inward conviction that she would one day be found by her father. That she was of high birth, Miss Sinclair could never feel a doubt, and her natural talents were excellent, so that the progress she made in the course of a few months was astonishing.

The gratitude of the young girl for the kindness shown her was unbounded, and she endeavoured by every little attention in her power to make some return to her benefactress, whose health seemed each day to become more and more delicate. She frequently lay awake all the first part of the night from incessant coughing, and generally fell asleep towards morning. Lily knew this, and therefore persuaded her to remain in bed until a late hour, and invariably paid her a visit before going out to her day's work, bringing a cup of warm tea and the small quantity of bread and butter she usually took for her breakfast.

One evening Miss Sinclair appeared so unusually feverish and excited that Lily was alarmed, and ran out to ask Biddy whether it would not be better to go and fetch the parish doctor, to see if he could administer anything to relieve her friend.

But Biddy shook her head, and said that it was quite useless to go for the parish doctor so late in the evening, he would be certain not to come until the next day, and perhaps not then. She went back with Lily to Miss Sinclair, and perceived at once that she was indeed much worse than usual, and therefore persuaded her to go to bed at once and take something warm, as she fancied she had a bad cold.

Both Lily and Biddy remained with Miss

Sinclair until a late hour, in fact, they did not leave her until she was comfortably asleep. Then they returned to their own home, and Lily left Miss Sinclair without anxiety, expecting to find her pretty well again the next morning. Biddy, however, felt uneasy. She had long known that the sick lady could not live long, for the priest, who went to visit the invalid almost daily, had told her so, and the great fear was her breaking a blood-vessel after violent coughing, and feverishness usually made her cough much worse. Biddy was anxious not to expose Lily to the chance of finding her friend dead, therefore she got up early and went out as far as Miss Sinclair's house, to ascertain whether the shutters were open, for when she was pretty well she always opened them early, that she might see the first dawn of daylight.

The shutters were all tightly closed, therefore she felt certain that Miss Sinclair must be very ill, and wished much to go into the house, but she knew by experience that it was useless to attempt such a thing at that early hour, as the other lodger would not open the door on any account until half-past six. Therefore she returned home, and when Lily got up and was dressed asked her to go to the market, which was at a good distance from her house, to purchase some apples she had seen there the day before. She begged her to go at once, lest any one else should buy them.

Lily prepared to go at once, but asked Biddy to take the cup of tea to Miss Sinclair in her place. Biddy promised to make a very nice one, and to take it to her directly the door was opened by the other lodger.

Lily hastened on her errand, and Biddy looked out again to see if Miss Sinclair's shutters were opened, but no, they were tightly closed, and she could not hear a sound in the house. At last, to her great relief, she saw the bony, gaunt figure of the lodger at her own window, which was the prelude to the door being opened. But the old body seemed in no hurry, and full ten minutes longer elapsed before the bolt was withdrawn from the entrance door.

Biddy entered quickly, and groped her way up the dark staircase. She knocked at the door of Miss Sinclair's room, but no answer was returned. She knocked, and knocked again, but in vain ; she tried to open the door, but could not succeed, there was something heavy lying against it, which prevented its being moved without more force being employed than she had strength for.

She went out into the street and called for assistance. Two men who were passing on their way to their day's work heard her, and came quickly to ask what the matter was. Biddy told them the case, and they followed her instantly, and soon forced open the door.

The obstacle which had prevented the door being opened was, as Biddy feared, the inanimate form of poor Miss Sinclair, who lay on the floor near it, quite dead. Apparently she had risen as usual to open her shutters, and the exertion had brought on a fit of coughing, which had caused her to break a blood-vessel.

Biddy and the two men lifted her up, and placed her on the bed, but life was quite extinct, although some warmth still remained in the hands.

Notwithstanding the suddenness of death, her countenance was so calm and placid that they felt sure she had died without pain or fear. A prayer-book was in her hand, she had probably been reading it before rising, as a candle was by the bedside.

Biddy rejoiced to think she had sent Lily to a distance, and thus saved the shock of finding her friend dead. She closed Miss Sinclair's eyes, arranged a white cap, which she found in one of the drawers, on her head, after placing the hair smoothly over her brow. She then clothed the corpse in a clean white dress, and replaced it on the bed which she had left alive a few hours before.

After putting everything neat and tidy in the room she went out, locking the door carefully, lest any one should enter to pilfer in her absence.

She took away a small desk containing letters and documents, which she guessed might be private papers which the poor deceased would not wish to be read by strangers. She could neither read or write herself, but she determined to let Lily look them over and see whether there were any wishes expressed which could be carried out.

She, however, put the desk away carefully in her own box, that Lily might not see it at first, as she was certain how terribly the young girl would feel the loss of her friend, but she thought that after the first burst of grief was over, it would be some consolation to her to carry out the last wishes of one whom she had loved so much. Biddy was an uneducated woman, but she had such a kind heart, that her natural impulse was to perform those acts of gentleness and amiability which are produced in others by the refined feelings consequent on early culture and careful education.

In the course of another hour Lily returned with her basket of apples. She was very tired, and in great want of food, but she wished to go and see Miss Sinclair before she touched the breakfast that Biddy had provided. The good woman, however, stopped her and said—

"Eat your breakfast first, my honey, I have been with Miss Sinclair more than an hour; she wants for nothing now, but is lying quietly on her bed."

Lily obeyed and sat down, but there was something in the expression of Biddy's face which made her uneasy; she did not smile as usual, and she looked as if she had been crying, as in truth she had. Lily could not eat much, and when she had finished that little got up and said—

"Now may I go and see Miss Sinclair? for I am certain by your face that she is very ill."

"Wait a bit, colleen!"

"Why must I wait? O dear Biddy! tell me the truth, is she very ill? is she dying?"

Biddy did not reply, but took Lily's small thin hand in her great bony claw, and said gently—

"You know, colleen, that you say every day, and many times in the day, 'Thy will be done,' and you really wish it when you say it, too!"

"O Biddy! O Biddy! it cannot be God's will for Miss Sinclair to die. Oh! say that she will get better—oh! *do* say that she will soon be better."

Biddy did not reply excepting with the words, "Thy will be done."

Lily guessed the truth at once; she could only falter out in a trembling voice—

"Let me see her, let me kneel by her side."

Biddy took two candles which had been given to her in the church, and which she kept for particular occasions and said—

"We will light these two candles, and place them by her side, and we will strew these white flowers on the bed."

Lily did not utter a word, but followed Biddy, and together they entered the chamber of death. They knelt by the side of the poor corpse, and although Lily wept silently, yet she was as quiet, as still as the corpse itself. She thought over all the lessons of goodness and conformity to the will of God inculcated by her friend, and she resolved to profit now by her words, and to submit patiently to this great grief and unexpected trial.

Biddy was astonished at her calmness, for the Irish are usually so demonstrative in their grief; she thought this calmness could not last, that it portended severe illness. But Lily left the room as quietly as she entered it, although no one could look at her sad sorrow-stricken face, without being certain how intensely she felt the death of her friend.

Biddy got quite alarmed at last at the calmness of Lily, and thought it best to endeavour to rouse her by bringing out the desk and papers of poor Miss Sinclair. But even this did not produce any outward demonstration of grief, for that desk, those papers, only reminded her still more of all that that pious lady had taught her.

They opened a small drawer in the desk, and found a letter in the handwriting of Miss Sinclair directed to Lily. It was short, but she told her how much she loved her; she said she was certain that her own life was nearly at an end, as she felt each day more and more weak. She begged Lily never to forget her, and to follow the advice she had given. She desired Lily to take possession of her few books and scanty wardrobe, and to give the only cloak she possessed to Biddy, as it was tidy although not very warm. She said she felt sure that God would one day give Lily the consolation of finding her father, and that her most fervent prayer in heaven should be for this, as it had been her constant one on earth.

The funeral took place very quickly, as the mistress of the lodging-house wished to let Miss Sinclair's room to some one else. Lily and Biddy followed her to her last resting-place. The grief of the former was demonstrative, that of the latter deep, but noiseless and uncomplaining.

CHAPTER XVI.

FRESH TRIALS AND ANXIETY.

ALMOST six months had passed by since the death of Miss Sinclair, and Lily had been nearly three years with the kind Irishwoman. She was contented and happy, as she loved her good friend, but the life she led was (as Biddy told her in the beginning) a hard one for a delicate young girl, whose appearance and form was that of one born for better things.

Although not sixteen, her height was that of a rather tall woman, but so slender that she seemed hardly able to support herself, much less carry a heavy basket. Her hands were small and delicate, notwithstanding the hard work she was compelled to do at Mrs. Heslope's, and far too white they were for health.

She was pale, very pale, although a rough word would bring colour quickly into her cheeks, but the bloom vanished as rapidly, and left her more white than before. She was ever gentle and sweet, and the happiest moments of the day were those she spent in the church, or among the sick, who were to be found in such numbers in the small court in which Biddy lived. She could not, of course, give them much help, as her kind benefactress was so poor, but she would go in the evening, when she returned from her day's work at the apple-stall, and make their kettle boil for a warm cup of tea, make their bed comfortable, speak words of hope and comfort, and sometimes read to them. All seemed to look up to her, young as she was, as something above them, almost as something not belonging to this world.

But each month Lily continued to feel less strong, less able to work, although her spirit kept her up, and she never uttered a word of complaint. Biddy, kind-hearted as she was, did not understand delicacy of constitution; she imagined that the only reason of Lily being so thin and pale was the fact of her growing so tall. From being a little deaf she did not hear the dry, hard cough which sometimes kept the weak young girl awake for hours at night, and as she never complained, but had always a sweet smile on her countenance, Biddy was quite free from any uneasiness. Neither did she know how much poor Lily suffered when trying to sell water-cress, how the rough, strong boys and girls, who had been brought up in the streets, made game of her, taunted her, and drove her from the places where she was likely to sell much by their coarse, wicked words, and sometimes even with blows, but she never answered, and would not tell Biddy, lest she should make her unhappy. She preferred anything, any suffering, to remaining at home and not adding her mite to the slender stock gained for their support. She suffered, likewise, terribly both from heat and cold; her weak constitution could not stand exposure to the sudden changes which are so trying in the English climate. Sometimes she got wet to the skin when endeavouring to sell fruit or water-cress, but she submitted cheerfully to everything, and got up early and walked miles in the cold, hoping to get purchasers for her cress before the other sturdy girls and boys commenced their rounds, for she was too timid to force her way anywhere, and when her tormentors appeared, ran away and hid herself, like a poor, frightened, hunted hare.

Months slipped by without much change, and it was again dark, dreary winter, and an unusually inclement one. The frost had set in with a cold, north-easterly wind early in November, and there was, from that time, a constant succession of deep snow and rapid thaws, which lasted only a few hours, and were followed by severe frosts. Every necessary of life was dear —coal, bread, and clothing. The season for fruit had been unfavourable, and it was, consequently, so difficult to get it at a moderate price, that Biddy was unable to lay in her usual stock for the winter. She could only purchase a little each week to sell again, and the profit she made was so small that want stared her in the face.

Ill and weak as Lily was, she did her utmost to gain something, but the water-cress was frozen up, and it was impossible to procure any to sell.

Good old Biddy never murmured, she continued to say, "May the blessed will of God be done." But at last, between starvation, cold, and want of proper clothing, she became so ill that she could not move, and was obliged to remain shivering in bed.

Lily was heart-broken at the sight of the sufferings of her good old friend. She determined to go at once to Father O'Hara to beg him to help them a little, but suddenly remembered, to her great sorrow, that he left London two days before to attend the dying bed of his mother in Ireland, and that the priest who had taken his place was a complete stranger to her, and had taken charge of the Mission for a month, at least. She knew no one in London but a few sick old men and women, and a few families who were in quite as much distress from the hard and bitter weather as themselves.

She did not like to leave good old Biddy alone, sick and suffering as she was,—but what was to be done? There was not a scrap of food in the house, no coal or wood to make a fire, and she did not possess a penny to purchase anything. Never in her life had she held out her hand to solicit charity, and her sensitive nature revolted at the bare idea of such a thing, but what could she do? How was it possible to see her good old friend perishing from want, without attempting something to procure the relief she so much needed. The apple stall was empty, and she had no means of renewing the stock, besides which it was late in the season, and apples were become so bad that it was difficult, if not impossible, to find purchasers. If she had only one shilling, and could purchase some winter violets, she would probably be able to sell them when made up into small nosegays, at a very considerable profit, as she had seen done by many girls in the market. But where to find this shilling? Ah! Lily! it was a hard struggle; however she put inclination on one side, offered the humiliation which duty demanded to our blessed Lord, and begged Him to give her the strength to do what was so repugnant to nature. She then turned to her old friend and said—

"I am going out, mother, for a bit; I will go to church and pray for you, and return soon, very soon."

She put on her hat and her shawl, thin enough it was, in truth, and little protection did it afford from the inclemency of the weather, but she thought of nothing, she hoped for nothing, but obtaining the means of relieving her dear, sick, starving benefactress.

Spanish Place Church was the nearest to her neighbourhood ; she soon reached it, entered, and knelt down in one of the last benches. Mass was commenced, she remained to the end, and spent the whole time imploring God to move the hearts of some of those assembled there to give her the relief she so much needed. She left the church directly Mass was ended, and stood outside the door studying the countenances of those who came out, and hoping that some among them would look upon her compassionately, speak, and thus give the courage required to beg relief. But each member of the congregation passed by hurriedly, every person seemed occupied with themselves, and only anxious to lose no time before commencing their daily occupations, whether of duty or of pleasure. She advanced timidly towards a fat, comely-looking, old lady, and was about to entreat her to bestow some small relief, when the old dame, burying her hands still deeper in the huge warm muff she was carrying, stopped all petitions by saying curtly—

"I never give to street beggars; do not stop me in this cold easterly wind."

Poor Lily said no more, but looked with longing eyes at the comfortable attire of the old lady, and wished in her own mind that she possessed something similar to put over the shivering form of good old Biddy.

One after another passed by, and at last Lily perceived, with a feeling of dismay, that all were gone save one old gentleman; his countenance had a grumpy expression, but she resolved to address him at all risks. She approached and said in a trembling voice—

"Kind sir, have compassion on me, I entreat you. Give me a trifle,—I am penniless, and my only friend in this world is lying sick, quite unable to move, at home."

"I make it a rule never to relieve beggars at church doors," answered the old gentleman sharply.

"Kind sir, do not refuse some small help," said the poor girl in a trembling voice, still holding out her hand.

"If you pester me any more, I will put you in charge of the police," growled the old gentleman testily, "get you gone, begging is a bad trade, go and work."

He bustled on as if fearful she might again address him, but he need not have feared, for his severe countenance and hard manner had utterly crushed the resolution of the timid young girl. He had a cold and cough apparently, and took out his handkerchief, as he walked away, to blow his nose, and unknown to himself pulled out with his handkerchief a loose shilling which was in his pocket,—it fell on the pavement, and rolled to the feet of despairing Lily. She instantly picked it up, and ran after the old gentleman, saying—

"You have just dropped this shilling, sir; you pulled it out of your pocket with your handkerchief."

"Lor bless us, what an absent chap I am. I suppose I tumbled my change loose in my pocket instead of putting it into my purse; here, give it to me, girl, quick. I have no time to wait."

Lily put the shilling into his hand. He looked at her, gave a little start, and said in a tone of surprise—

"Are not you the girl who was begging from me at the church door just now?"

"Yes, sir, I implored you to give me a trifle to provide necessaries for the only friend I have on earth, who is ill, and perhaps dying."

"Why did you not keep this shilling?"

"It was not mine, sir; you dropped it by mistake, you had not given it to me."

"But I did not know I had dropped it, you might have kept it, and no one would have been the wiser."

"But Almighty God would have known it, sir. He would have been displeased at my dishonesty, and I would not do anything to displease Him for all the gold or silver in the world, destitute and starving as I am."

The old gentleman looked both surprised and touched.

"Well, you do seem to be an honest, good girl," he said. "You shall have this shilling, and another too, to reward your honesty."

"Oh! thank you, sir; I shall then be able to purchase necessaries for my dear sick friend, and do other things besides."

He put the two shillings in her thin wasted hand, and was about to ask questions as to where she lived, that he might give her more assistance if he found she really required it (he being in truth a kind-hearted old man); but he disliked beggars at church doors, and had seen so much of the imposture of street beggars, that he rarely bestowed anything upon them. However, just as he was about to speak, he was seized with such a fit of coughing and sneezing that he could not utter a word, and Lily, who did not understand his kind intentions, walked off as fast as possible with the two shillings in her hand, anxious to purchase some food for the destitute apple-woman.

She bought a little tea and sugar, a nice penny roll, a faggot, a small measure of coal, and a little bit of tobacco. In these things, and a penny loaf for herself, she expended one shilling, and hastened home joyfully with her little load. She found the old woman still very ill, but she lighted the fire, boiled some water, and soon made a nice warm cup of tea, which she persuaded her to take with a slice of roll.

These comforts revived the good old woman somewhat, and she thanked Lily most warmly, more especially when she found that she had likewise provided a little tobacco.

"Now that you are more comfortable, granny" (the pet name by which she called the old woman), "I will go out to buy some violets with my remaining shilling, which I shall make into small nosegays, and try to sell to ladies. I have been told that at this season of the year you may make considerable profit—I can but try."

"Go, then, my honey; and may the blessing of God be wid you."

Lily went quickly to a large green-grocer's shop. She purchased a handful of violets and a nice bunch of green leaves for her shilling, and brought them home, where she divided the whole into twelve packets, to tie up into twelve little bunches. She calculated that if she sold each bunch for twopence, she should have a shilling of profit to spend on the suffering apple-woman. Before tying them up, however, she subtracted one violet from each packet to make an extra bunch to put on the altar of Spanish Place Church, as a thank-offering for the assistance she had obtained from the old gentleman at that church door.

She tied all her bunches up neatly, and arranged them carefully in her basket so as to look pretty and tempting, and then set off, determined to do her best to sell them quickly.

But she soon found, alas! that it was not as easy to sell as to purchase the violets,—it was rather late in the day, ladies who wished for flowers had already procured them from large shops when they first came in in the morning fresh from the country.

She walked down a great part of Oxford Street without finding a purchaser for even one bunch; there were many other girls with baskets of flowers there, who sold them more readily than she did, because they had no timidity, none of the natural bashfulness of Lily. They went boldly up to the carriages, thrust their flowers in at the windows, and to stop their importunity the ladies sometimes purchased flowers that they did not wish for, while timorous Lily held her basket at a distance, not daring to approach or force her flowers on them.

One fashionably-attired young man took a bunch, saying that a look at her blue eyes was worth more than the twopence she charged for the nosegay. He tossed the price into her basket, but she was frightened at his bold unblushing gaze, bent her head, and walked away as fast as possible.

She next held her basket to two prim-looking old maids, who turned over every flower, not caring how much they spoiled them, and forced her to sell two very good bunches for three halfpence, which they said was much more than the flowers were worth.

Sick at heart, and quite discouraged, the poor girl directed her steps through Portman Square into Harley Street. In that street she was rather more fortunate, for a fat cook who was standing at the gate of an area, looking about, purchased two bunches at twopence each. She was a good-natured old soul too, that cook, for she looked at Lily's dejected countenance and thin hands, and said—

"Wait a bit, my girl, you look hungry, I will give you a bit of the plum-pudding we had for dinner yesterday."

She went into her kitchen and brought forth a huge lump which she deposited in the basket of flowers.

Lily received it with grateful thanks, and said she would carry it home. The cook looked disappointed, as she expected to see the young girl devour it at once; however, being kind-hearted, she thought inwardly that she might prefer eating it at home and sharing it with her sick friend. The fat healthy cook could not imagine any one being unable to eat such a nice morsel; she did not know that poor Lily was, indeed, far too sick to do more than look at the rich, heavy, cold pudding. Such, however, was not the case with an urchin down the street, who saw the pudding in Lily's basket a few minutes afterwards.

His eyes perfectly expanded with pleasure at the sight of what he considered such a delicious treat, and when she took it out of her basket and put it into his hand he commenced devouring it with such avidity, that even sad, dejected Lily could not restrain a laugh at his delight, and the hearty manner in which he shouted out at the top of his voice—

" Oh ! my eyes, how good !—first-rate,—thank 'e, but didn't 'e want some ye self?"

However, in two minutes the whole was gone.

She next met a lady who was leading a delicate-looking little boy. He turned to his mother beseechingly, and said—

"O mamma, dear, do give some pennies to that poor, pale girl; I am sure she is sick as I was last year. Oh! do, mamma, please, give me something for her.

The mother gave the child all the halfpence she had in her pocket, which was only twopence; he put them in Lily's hand joyfully, thinking they were quite a large fortune.

The day, however, was passing by quickly, it was beginning to get dusk, she had not sold half her bunches, they were becoming faded and less likely to be purchased, and she had not even regained the shilling spent on them. She had heard some flower-girls say that if they went in the evening and stood by large houses where a carriage was at the door waiting to convey the ladies of the family to some place of amusement or evening party, and took that opportunity of presenting the basket at the carriage door, they were pretty certain of having a good sale for the flowers. She determined to try this plan, turned down Marylebone Street, and walked on to Portland Place, where the houses are large, and the inmates rich.

The large Langham Hotel stood at one end of Portland Place on her right hand, it was brilliantly lighted up, but she did not direct her steps in that direction, feeling very certain that it was useless to go there, as she would be driven from the doors very quickly by the busy waiters.

It had been snowing during a great part of

the morning, in the afternoon there was a partial thaw, but towards five o'clock a sharp frost again set in, therefore the pavement was excessively slippery. Lily feared every moment that she should lose her footing and fall down, but anxiety to procure some relief for Biddy made her persevere in her efforts to get on. She saw a carriage on the opposite side, which was standing at the door of a large house, she immediately crossed over, placed herself near that door, and stood shivering with her basket of faded violets in her hands.

In a few moments it was opened, a carpet was brought out, and spread from the hall door of this house to the carriage door. This sight gave her fresh courage, she felt certain that the carpet must be spread for some lady to walk on, to get into her carriage, and she hoped that the sight of her emaciated limbs, would move a gentle lady to compassion, therefore she waited, although her thin hands and feet ached so with cold that she could scarce endure the pain.

She waited five or six minutes, when at length an elegant form, attired in a rich black velvet dress, appeared at the door and passed so swiftly along the carpet, and sprang so lightly into the carriage, that she did not even see poor Lily, who endeavoured in vain to attract her attention. Another figure now came to the door, a lady tastefully attired in a costly pink silk dress, with a wreath of flowers around her luxuriant and glossy fair hair. She likewise passed as swiftly as possible from the door to her carriage, followed by poor Lily, who endeavoured to approach close with her basket to offer up her petition, but she was rudely shoved on one side by the footman, who said roughly—

"Get you gone, girl, you and your dirty basket, or I will call a policeman."

Despair gave Lily courage, she stood still, she would not move, but raised her plaintive voice and exclaimed, in touching accents, so as to be heard by the two ladies in the carriage—

"For the love of God, I implore you, dear ladies, to have pity on me, to help me."

The footman was enraged at her pertinacity, he gave her a shove on one side, and she, worn out with cold and hunger, was unable from weakness to save herself, she staggered, the basket dropped from her hands, and she fell down on the pavement, her head struck against a curb stone with such force as to render her totally insensible.

The footman, either believing, or fancying he believed her to be drunk, banged the carriage door, jumped on the box, and was telling the coachman to drive on, when the check string was violently pulled by one of the persons in the carriage, and the voice of the lady in the black velvet dress was heard exclaiming in an anxious tone—

"Do not drive on, William ; get down, James, instantly, and come here."

The footman obeyed, and approached the carriage window.

"Who is that poor girl who was asking charity, and whom you pushed away and knocked down before I had time to speak to her ? "

"Please, 'um, she's only one of them there flower-girls, what's had a drop too much. I only touched her arm, and down she went like a stone, as they always do when they're drunk,— there, get up, girl, at once, will 'e ? there, be quick ! "

The unfortunate girl remained totally insensible on the flags where she had fallen, and no pushes had any effect in arousing her.

"It is not true," said the lady in pink, "I am certain that the beseeching cry I heard was not the voice of a tipsy person, it was a wail of distress; and you, James, you were not moved by her distress, you have killed the poor unfortunate girl. I am very certain she is dead, look at her white cheeks, look at her lean wan countenance!"

James was not really hard-hearted, but he had seen much of street imposture, and being very cross at having to go out with the carriage on such a bitterly cold night, he had acted and spoken with more brutality than was in his nature. The gentle words of his mistress aroused feelings of remorse, he looked with more compassion at the motionless form before him, and endeavoured to raise her gently from the ground, but although he could easily lift the young girl, he could not restore consciousness,—her arms were stiff, and her head fell powerlessly on his arm.

He was now really frightened, he made sure he had killed her, and mentally resolved to show more compassion in future to the needy and distressed.

Both the ladies, despite the cold wind and bitter frost, got out of the carriage, and were quite moved to tears, as they looked at the unknown but suffering girl; they called the butler, and requested him to assist the footman in carrying her into their own house.

The butler, who was a kind-hearted man and had children of his own, came out quickly, and they soon carried Lily through the front hall into a comfortable small room at the other end, where she was placed on the sofa, and they then sent at once for the doctor.

He did not arrive for more than half an hour, but in the meantime the two benevolent ladies did all in their power to restore the fainting girl to consciousness,—by bathing her temples with eau-de-Cologne, and pouring a little wine down her throat.

They looked with pity at her scanty clothing, and wondered that thus slightly clad she should have ventured out on such an inclement night. They marvelled at finding that her coarse, patched, tattered under-garments were clean, and all neatly put together. They glanced at her thin white hands and feet, and remarked with surprise that their form was that of one of gentle blood, totally unlike the thick stumpy hands and feet of those brought up to gain their livelihood by hawking goods in the public streets. They felt quite sad, and contrasted their own warm rich attire with the poverty and wretchedness of the little sufferer, now lying motionless and as if dead before them, almost without stockings, so very thin they were, and with shoes so worn and filled with holes that they afforded no protection to her feet from the wet and the bitter cold.

But these kind ladies had no real cause for self-reproach on that head, for they were only dressed as their position in life required, and neither the one nor the other ever turned a deaf ear to the call of distress. They rarely indulged themselves in the purchase of anything that could be called a superfluity, and they were ever ready to open their purses, and subscribe to the utmost of their means to public charities when required, besides which their private donations were unbounded, and many were the prayers offered up for them by the widow and the orphan.

They kept up a large establishment, and lived in a style suitable to the position of the husband of the elder lady, and this was in accordance with his wishes, as he considered that keeping up a large household, and spending money freely in all ways, was a praiseworthy employment of wealth, inasmuch as it encouraged trade, and was even a greater charity than distributing food to the starving, as it enabled thousands to provide comfortably for themselves and their families, instead of applying to others for relief.

The doctor came at last, and administered a cordial to the fainting girl, which restored consciousness, but he shook his head, said she was very weak, and recommended her being sent as soon as possible to some hospital, as, from her appearance, he feared she could not live many weeks, perhaps even not many days. He said that she was delicately formed (unusually so), and appeared to have suffered the most fearful want and exposure to the inclement weather.

The lady of the house immediately proposed that she should be sent to St. Elizabeth's Hospital, as her husband, being a large subscriber to that most useful and well-regulated institution, had the disposal of one bed there, which bed chanced at that time to be vacant. At that hospital she would have not only the attendance of the best medical practitioners, but also the tender and motherly nursing of the pious nuns who had charge of the patients. They felt sure that the young girl was a Catholic, because they had remarked that directly consciousness returned, she instinctively put her hand to her forehead and made the sign of the Cross, as if awaking from a sound sleep in the early morn, and murmured, almost inarticulately, short ejaculatory prayers.

It was therefore determined that she should be conveyed to St. Elizabeth's Hospital as soon as possible, and the two benevolent ladies deferred going to the evening party until their carriage should have returned from taking her there. They sent their own maid also in the carriage, and covered Lily with a large and very warm shawl; they put a bottle of hot water at the bottom of the carriage and persuaded her to swallow a little nice warm soup.

Had the ladies followed the kind impulse of their hearts they would have taken her to the hospital themselves; but the drive was a long one, the night bitterly cold, and both having very delicate constitutions, they did not dare run the risk of the cold draughts to which they might be exposed in getting in and out of the carriage and walking through the sick wards.

The carriage reached the hospital, and in the course of half-an-hour Lily was placed in a very warm and comfortable bed in one of the wards, with a kind and devoted nun to nurse her, and carry out every direction given by the doctor.

She felt as if she must be in heaven, and thanked and blessed God for sending her such humane and charitable friends in her distress; but she could not rest quietly until she had begged the nursing nun to send a message to the sick applewoman to say what had happened, and she entreated them likewise to send a little food, as Biddy would, if not assisted, starve— being so ill, unable to work, and now deprived of her assistance also.

The nuns instantly asked the consent of the Superioress, which was cheerfully given, and a messenger was despatched with a basket containing tea, sugar, biscuits, and a small bit of bacon, which gifts had been left that morning, by a charitable lady, for the use of the needy.

Lily was perfectly overjoyed when these things were sent to her sick friend, and she thanked the good nuns over and over again.

They told her to keep her mind easy, and try to go to sleep, as they would look after Biddy constantly, until she herself was quite well again and able to return to her stall, therefore that she must not be anxious on account of her valued old friend.

CHAPTER XVII.

SCENE IN PORTLAND PLACE.

FOUR persons were seated at a comfortable breakfast table in the dining-room of the large house, in Portland Place, at the door of which Lily had met with her sad accident on the previous evening.

These four persons were the lady and gentleman of the house, her sister (who lived with them), and a nephew, who was paying them a visit of a few weeks. A fifth place was laid, but it was unoccupied, and there was much discussion among those seated at table, as to the cause of the absence of the missing guest.

"What an incomprehensible character," said the mistress of the house, addressing her nephew, "your friend seems to be; he is totally unlike any person I have ever before met. At times you think him both eccentric and severe, and regard him with fear; but the next moment you see on his countenance a look of patience and resignation which is truly touching ; he rarely, or never smiles—I cannot make him out at all. Perhaps I should understand him better if we were more intimate, I might then possibly get to like him. What is your opinion, Charley ? "

" I esteem him, my dear aunt, more than any other person I am acquainted with in this world, but well may you consider his character incomprehensible. I have known him several years, and yet I can scarcely say that I understand him better than you do. The thing in creation of which he constantly reminds me, is the beautiful annual called the 'convolvulus.' If you look at this plant at mid-day, or in the afternoon, or evening, you see nothing but dark sombre green leaves, and faded dead blossoms. You wonder how any person of taste could allow such a dirty, shabby plant to remain among the beautiful and gay flowers with which the garden is filled, you quite long to root it up, —but if you look again by chance the next morning at an early hour, to your astonishment you behold the despised plant covered with flowers of various colours so beautiful, so bright, so elegant, that you look from one to the other, without knowing which to prefer, and you pronounce this plant to be the most lovely in the garden. The refreshing night dew, and the cheering bright morning light, have made this sudden change in its appearance; the bright-coloured flowers were always there, but folded up and hidden so closely as to deceive the eye, and make the beholder believe that there was really nothing but dark green leaves. So it is with the character of my friend; at times he seems so silent, so absent, so absorbed in his own thoughts, that you fancy no fine qualities exist, but if a case of need, a person in affliction, or something of that kind is brought before him, it has the same effect in bringing out the fine qualities in his character as the dew and the clear morning light have on the convolvulus flowers—they unfold, one after another, and you are at a loss which to admire most. He told me, last night, that he intended going to the early service at the church in Farm Street, as he had an appointment afterwards with one of the Fathers, who had promised to inquire into the truth of a case of destitution which had been mentioned to him by chance. As prudence is necessary in London, where mendicity is a trade, and the impositions so frequent, he preferred asking the Fathers about it first, as they are acquainted with most of the poor in the parish, and cannot be easily deceived. I have no doubt that this is the cause of his want of punctuality, for the person he was to see may have been called out unexpectedly to some one near death, and thus prevented keeping the appointment he made with my friend. But I fancy I hear the front door bell, it may be him."

The hall door was quickly opened, the stranger entered, and after apologising for his want of punctuality, said that Father G—— was not able to see him immediately, but that when he did at last come, he had begged earnestly that he would lose no time in going to the locality where the poor family in question dwelt, as it was a case of most urgent distress, and although he had given them a trifle which he happened to have in his pocket, yet the destitution was still most terrible.

"Therefore, dear madam," he said, addressing the mistress of the house, "I trusted that you would kindly excuse my coming in late for breakfast, and I directed my steps instantly towards the court designated by Father G——."

The stranger pronounced these words with such a winning smile and expression of benevolence on his countenance, that every one at table thought of Charley's comparison of the convolvulus, and the lady addressed responded courteously—

"Pray do not think in the least about the slight delay; our only fear in the matter was lest your health should suffer from being so long without food, as you left the house quite early this morning. But you must satisfy our curiosity regarding this case of distress, whilst I pour out a hot cup of coffee for you."

The stranger returned his best thanks and said—

"It would harrow your tender feelings far too much if I described minutely all the particulars of this sad case. But imagine a whole family crowded together in one small attic without fire, almost without clothing, and without the means of purchasing food. The father (whose earnings usually kept the family) had been seized with rheumatic fever brought on by a chill, and was lying powerless, stretched out on a bit of sacking, with scarcely a rag to cover him; his wife, who had been lately confined, sat by his side, with a poor miserable baby in her arms, and three other children were crouched in different parts of the room. The cry which assailed my ears when I entered that sad dwelling, I shall not easily forget. 'Bread! bread! give my children bread, give my husband, my dear, good, dying husband something to cover him from the bitter cold. Oh! have pity on us, have pity on us, as you hope that God will have pity on you.' I was, as you may believe, affected beyond measure by these heartrending cries, and I left the room without delay to make a few purchases to relieve the immediate wants of the family. This, of course, took up some time, and has been the cause of that delay which you have so kindly forgiven."

"Forgiven, indeed," answered the master of the house promptly, "who would not rejoice at a delay caused by an act of charity which Providence gave you the happiness of performing. We can only envy you the privilege, and when you have refreshed yourself a little, my wife shall, in her turn, give you an account of a most interesting case of great need which kind Providence placed in our hands yesterday evening."

The stranger begged to hear about it at once, and the ladies soon gave him a description of Lily's accident at their door. He listened to the narration with the greatest interest, and when they said they intended to go that morning to St. Elizabeth's Hospital to visit the patient sufferer, he begged to be allowed to accompany them to see her, and likewise to go over the rest of the hospital, of which he had heard so much. He had been told by many persons that it was one of the best organised institutions in London, and that the invalids enjoyed every possible advantage, both spiritual and temporal, having high and airy rooms, devoted nuns to nurse them, and the attendance of some of the best medical practitioners in London. He likewise asked whether it was true that the sick inmates could see into the church, and hear Mass, by opening a window, when they were confined to their beds by illness.

He was answered in the affirmative on each point, and both ladies said they should be delighted to take him with them. As the carriage was ordered at eleven o'clock, he might go over the whole hospital and judge for himself, and he could likewise accompany them into the ward where Lily was, and see the interesting young girl.

The stranger thanked them for their kindness, and said he would be ready punctually at the time they had named. Eleven o'clock struck, James announced the carriage, both ladies sprang lightly into it, followed by the stranger, and in less than half-an-hour they stopped at the entrance of St. Elizabeth's Hospital.

CHAPTER XVIII.

ST. ELIZABETH'S HOSPITAL.

THE two benevolent ladies, accompanied by the stranger, soon entered the hospital, where the former were well known, as they visited it frequently. The Superioress soon conducted them to the sick ward where Lily had been made so comfortable on the previous evening, and the compassionate ladies went up to the bed of the weak sufferer, stood by it, and gently took her thin white hand, whispering at the same time words of sympathy, to which she responded, and smiled sweetly.

The stranger, as agreed upon, went to the head of the bed, where he could see and hear the feeble invalid without being seen himself.

But why! when she raised her weak voice to thank the ladies for their kindness, did he start as if he had heard a clap of thunder? Why did his stout and stalwart frame shake suddenly as one struck with palsy? Why did that strong, that brave-looking man, turn almost as white as the sheets of the bed on which the gentle sufferer rested? Why was he forced to take hold of the bed-post to prevent falling? And why did he look at that pale-faced child as if he was contemplating a spectre?

The two ladies and the nuns regarded him in astonishment, but he spoke not a word, he remained as if riveted to the spot where he stood.

The silence remained unbroken for a few moments, and Lily closed her eyes and seemed to doze. The stranger then stepped forward for an instant, looked at the pale sleeper, and muttered in a hoarse whisper—

"Oh! my God! my God! it is my child, the very image of her mother."

He glanced at the little miniature which was lying on her bosom, and again such a thrill seemed to pass over him that he must have fallen, had not the good nun and the elder of the two ladies supported, and almost against his will led him out of the sick ward into the adjoining room. There he sank on a chair, and wept as few men have wept before, and exclaimed in broken sentences—

"Oh! my God! my God! and I only find my lost one to see her die. Oh! my God, save her, or, if die she must, let her recognise and give me one look of affection before she expires. Let me at least receive her last breath, and close those eyes which I have so long thought of, and longed, oh! how I have longed, to look upon once again."

The two ladies thought he must be in delirium, but not so the elder of the two nuns, who had heard from Lily fragments of her sad history, and had seen the small portrait she always wore concealed in her bosom.

This nun at once recognised the unmistakable resemblance of the portrait to the agitated stranger. She approached him and said gently—

"You are not mistaken. This poor sick girl is doubtless your little Lily, your lost one! Thank God for granting the prayer she has so long offered up of being allowed to see you, and receive your last blessing and the assurance of your love, before she leaves this earth, which has been so sad, and so full of trial for her; but you must be prudent, as the doctor says that any sudden joy, or sudden sorrow, might snap the frail thread, on which her life hangs, in a moment. Therefore, listen to my words. Return home, calm yourself down to complete conformity to the Divine Will, and wait until I send for you. It shall be my pleasing task to prepare the mind of this dear child, to see you with calmness once, at least, before her pure soul takes flight to that happy land where pain, and tears, and anxieties are no more. Do not hesitate," she continued, seeing the stranger cast a longing glance at the door of the room in which he had left his child,—" do not hesitate, but obey me at once."

She pronounced these words in a tone which showed that from high and conscientious motives she was determined to be obeyed, and opened the door which led to the passage by which they entered.

The stranger arose, and as if fascinated by some incomprehensible spell, obeyed, and walked out of the room without uttering a syllable, followed by the two ladies, who offered to send for their carriage immediately, for him to return home. He gladly availed himself of their kindness; for he was so unnerved as to be totally unable to walk any distance, but when seated by their side in the carriage he said not a word, and no one ventured to ask an explanation of the extraordinary scene they had witnessed.

After the departure of the stranger and the ladies, Sister Placida returned to the bedside of Lily, whom she had left sleeping. She still slept, but her slumber was light, though calm. She soon awoke, looked up at the Sister, and said in a joyful tone—

"O Sister Placida! dear Sister Placida! I have had such a sweet dream. I saw my angel guardian standing by my side. His eyes were bright as a sunbeam, and his beautiful wings were spread out as if prepared for flight. He leaned over me, and he spoke to me. His voice was soft and low as the sound of distant music on a calm summer eve, and he whispered—

"'Rejoice! be glad, my child, your trials are at an end, and the prayer which has been so often presented for you at the throne of the Most High is granted!'

"I longed to hear more, and gazed enraptured with his beauty. I listened with all the powers of my soul, but as I gazed he vanished from my sight, even as a morning mist, or a light cloud. He signed me to follow him, and his words remained indelibly impressed on my heart. I am passing away, Sister, but I am certain that our Lord has heard, and has granted my prayer."

"What prayer, dear child?"

"O Sister Placida, my prayer each day since I lost my sweet mother has been, that Mary the Mother of mercy would obtain for me the comfort, the happiness of seeing my dear father once, at least, before I die. I feel certain that he is not dead, and that the prayer of so many years is granted; that I shall, before death, see him once more."

"Should you recognise him, dear child, if you did see him, after the lapse of so many years?"

"Oh yes! I am certain I should; I have so continually thought of him, I have so constantly looked at the little miniature which I have worn for so many years. It was his parting gift, he told me to keep it always. I laughingly told him that I would, that I would love it as I did my own dear pappy! I said this with childish unconsciousness and mirth, little thinking that I was going to lose him for ever, that I should lose my sweet mother too, and that this picture would be my only consolation for so many years. Oh yes, dear Sister, I should recognise him in a moment, and I should bless and thank God for giving me this consolation. I should die so happily, dear Sister, for I have no wish to live; my life has been a constant scene of misery and suffering, with few bright intervals, but I bless God for every trial He has sent me. He has supported me through all; He has, by His grace, preserved me from great offences, and now He will receive me into His arms, to be happy for all eternity, and when I am in heaven my constant prayer will be for my dear father. But yet I should like to see him once before I die, to know that he still loves me, then I should be happy, quite happy."

She looked up sweetly at the gentle nun, and then perceived that another person was by her bedside. It was the good priest who attended the hospital, and who had again been sent for after the visit of the doctor.

"My dear child," he said, "I am come to see you. Do you feel a little stronger than when I saw you last night?"

"No, Father, I am much weaker, I feel as if life was fast passing away. May I not soon receive the last sacraments?"

"Yes, my child, you may prepare at once, for you are quite right in thinking that you are sinking fast. The doctor says that he does not believe you will live many days, perhaps even not many hours. But I am sure you are quite resigned to the Divine will; you do not regret life?"

"Oh no, dear Reverend Father, indeed I do not. May the blessed will of God be done in all things, and yet, although I wish to desire nothing that is not God's will, I still pray that I may see my father before I die, if but once only. Pray for me—pray for me."

"My child, you must now put these thoughts and wishes out of your mind, think only of preparing for eternity. You may make your confession, and you shall then receive our dear Lord into your heart, probably for the last time, think only of giving Him a proper welcome. You are so near death that you may receive holy Communion without delay, after which I will administer the sacrament of Extreme Unction, which will give you the strength and grace necessary to support you in your passage out of this life into a better. So prepare for confession at once, dear child, and the effort will not fatigue you much, as it is such a short time, as you said last night (when we thought you were dying), since your last confession and Communion."

He put on his stole and seated himself by the bed of the dying girl, and when she had finished her confession, said a few fervent prayers to help her to prepare for holy Communion, and she remarked with gratitude and pleasure that among the graces and blessings which he implored our Lord to grant her, he mingled petitions that she might be allowed to see her father once, at least, before death. She joined in these prayers with the greatest fervour, and continued them mentally, when she had received her dear Lord.

After a short period of silence and recollection, he told her that she should now receive Extreme Unction, and that the two ladies who had been so kind to her wished to be present, if she thought their being in the room would not agitate her.

"Oh no," she answered promptly, "oh no,

indeed, they have been angels of comfort to me; had it not been for their kindness I should have died in the workhouse, with scarcely a religious comfort, instead of being surrounded by these dear holy nuns, and in the enjoyment of every possible spiritual blessing. Let them come in, that I may thank and assure them that when God in His goodness admits me to heaven, my most fervent prayer (after that for my dear father) shall be offered up for them."

The ladies entered the room softly, and stood by the bed. Lily tried to speak, but her previous words had exhausted the small stock of strength remaining in her; she, however, looked at them and smiled, and it was a heavenly, a placid smile.

The stranger came into the room too, but he knelt where he could not be seen.

The priest then commenced the sacred rites, —he anointed each member by which she might have offended God, and implored Him by His tender mercy to pardon every fault committed. When all was over she raised her eyes but lay perfectly still, placid as an angel. No one spoke for some time. At last a nun approached, offered her a cordial, and asked how she felt.

"Oh! better, much better, dear Sister. I feel as if strength was returned, almost as if I might recover; but I do not wish that, my only link to life is the thought that if I lived a little longer I might see my father once more."

"Should you be content then, my child?"

"Oh yes, I should die in perfect peace. My father would know that his child has never ceased loving him, and praying for his return; he would think of me happy, as I now am; he would know that I have tried to love and serve God; he would know that sorrow and mourning were passed for me, and he would look forward, after a few years of exile here below, to joining my mother and myself among the lovely bright spirits above, in our true and lasting home."

"But would it not agitate you, my child, to see him, now that you are so near your end?"

"Oh no; if my dear father was by my side, if he put his hand gently on my head, as he used in former days, I should feel as if I was once more a young child seated on my mother's knee, listening to the beautiful tales she used to tell of the angels and saints, and the love of our Lord for us, and the happy deaths of the saints. I should pass out of this life so peacefully, so calmly, yes, indeed, I should."

The nun made a sign to the stranger to approach. He did so, he stood for a moment before her. She did not start, she did not utter a sound, but the expression of her face showed that she recognised him instantly, and a seraphic smile of gratitude and delight lighted up her poor, extenuated, pale countenance. He leant over her, he placed his hand on her head, and said in a voice almost choking from emotion—

"God bless you, my own sweet Lily, my lost one, my loved child, for whom I have mourned for so many sad years. God bless you with His choicest blessings,—oh, my child! my only child."

She looked at him with inexpressible tenderness and love, and whispered—

"Thank God! I die happy. Do not mourn, we shall soon meet again in heaven."

The priest took her hand, felt her pulse, and knew that life was ebbing fast,—he commenced the touching prayers for a departing soul, in which all joined.

The stranger knelt by the bed, holding the hand of his dying child, and looking at her as if he would snatch her from the hands of death. She fixed her eyes upon him lovingly and peacefully. Suddenly a bright smile lighted up her countenance, she closed her eyes, and was gone! Not a struggle, not a sigh escaped her, it seemed as if she had dropped asleep, like a babe in the arms of its mother.

But they saw she no longer breathed, and the poor afflicted father stretched out his hand, closed her eyes, and impressed a kiss on that cold, pale cheek. And then he hid his face in his hands, and his sobs could no longer be repressed, they burst forth with such appalling force that the bed against which he leant vibrated and shook like a ship in a storm. He had restrained himself for a time lest he should disturb his child, but now, she was gone! he was again alone, a bereaved, a heart-broken parent, and his feelings of loneliness and misery were beyond expression.

The compassionate priest uttered words of comfort, but they fell like rain on a hard turnpike road, they refreshed the surface for a moment, and then every trace was gone.

The good nun, too, spoke sweetly and calmly, and bade him thank God for having granted the prayer of his child, and for the happiness of her last moments.

But he looked at her with a vacant, miserable smile, and did not reply.

At last she remembered that Lily had given her a small sealed packet, with the charge, that if ever her father was discovered, to give it to him, and say that it contained the last wishes of his loved and lost child. He took it with a trembling hand, and opened it.

The words it contained were few, but they were most touching. She conjured him, if he had not forgotten his child, to grant her dying request, which was to do his utmost, if he had the means, to found an institution for the relief of poor children, who, like herself, having been deprived by death, or some other mischance, of their parents and friends, and are left unprotected, homeless, and unprovided for in this pitiless world after having been in childhood accustomed to every comfort.

"Do this, my beloved father," she wrote, "and the happiness such a good work will bring to your heart, will be full compensation for all that you have, I doubt not, suffered on my account. In the love and gratitude of those unprotected little ones, you will find compensation for the trial you have had in being deprived of your own wife and child."

The stranger was inexpressibly touched by the letter, but uttered not a word. He cast his eyes upon a beautiful crucifix near the bed, arose, and walked slowly to the convent church. He entered, walked up to the altar, and throwing himself on his knees, exclaimed—

"Lord, I accept this from Thy hands, and entirely resign myself to Thy will. Yes, yes, I accept this, even this, the greatest, the most bitter of my trials, and I will carry out the wish of my child."

He remained before the altar for almost an hour, thanking and blessing God, first, for having allowed him to see his child before her death, and secondly, for having preserved her in her innocence, and then taken her to heaven to be happy for ever.

The stranger arose from his prayer with a changed countenance—hope and love had taken the place of despair and morose misery, and he returned to the room he had left.

During his absence the nuns had performed the last sad offices. Lily was attired in her white shroud, and they had placed a wreath of sweet roses and lilies around her head. The expression of her countenance was not in the least changed, there was still the smile which had lighted it up just before death, and the same look of peace and happiness which had played over it like a sunbeam.

The afflicted father gazed intently on his child, so intently that he did not perceive at first that he was not alone, that another person had entered the room just before the death of Lily.

This person was a grey-headed old priest, who approached and introduced himself as the parish priest of the locality where Biddy lived; the priest to whom the departed girl had had recourse so constantly for spiritual advice and help during the time she lived with the old apple-woman. Had he not been absent in Ireland attending the dying bed of his mother, she would have had recourse to him in her great distress, and he would have assisted her, but the Ecclesiastic he left in his place had an abrupt manner, and she feared him.

Father O'Brian (for that was the name of the old priest) had heard of her illness and death at the same moment, on his return home, and hastened to the hospital to hear the particulars as soon as possible. He took the hand of the sorrowing father, he pressed it kindly, and said in a feeling and gentle tone—

"Weep not, weep not, afflicted father, for although the cross selected by our Lord for you to bear after Him seems heavy, seems to you, in fact, almost insupportable, yet there is so much cause for thankfulness, so much cause even to rejoice, that I say again, Weep not, weep no more. I knew your dear child, I revered her wonderful purity and innocence, but when I heard suddenly of her impending death, I could only rejoice, I could not heave a sigh. A moment's reflection was sufficient to make me thank God from the very depths of my soul, for having removed her from the sorrows, the trials of this world. And even now that I know that the greatest part of these griefs would have been ended, I still say as I did at first, rejoice, rejoice that she is called to mingle with the gentle, guileless, lovely kindred spirits above. Among the children of innocence, light, and joy, she will be at home, and in her proper place. Unsuited was she for this world, its ways she did not understand; the existence of evil, in its most common forms, she appeared unable to comprehend; where others saw evil plainly and fully, she could hardly be brought to suspect; and where others condemned without scruple, she could scarce venture to fear. Great innocence and great humility seem ill-sorted companions, but they met in her. The little she enjoyed of happiness she found in the happiness of others, never more delighted than when she could ease the sufferings or contribute to the comfort of her neighbours. I shall offer the Holy Mass for her intention, as I promised long ago, if it pleased God to call her suddenly from this world, but she cannot need suffrages, for if the humble are to be exalted, if the pure of heart are to see God, if the merciful are to find mercy, she cannot but be in bliss. Well, however, can I understand, bereaved parent, what you must suffer at the present moment, to find your lost one only to lose her again for ever in this world. You feel as if your life henceforth, without even the hope of recovering your child, must be a dreary, weary blank, like a dismal day without hope of seeing the sun, or a dark night without even a glimmering star. But if life is a blank henceforth, the cross is doubly beneficial, for while it makes the eternal happiness of your child quite secure beyond the reach of any possibility of disturbance, it goes a very long way towards securing your own salvation. He to whom this life is a blank, ought to be grateful for that which has contributed to make it such, for slight, indeed, is his danger or chance of losing life eternal. The more thoroughly we are disengaged from this world, and disgusted with it, the more we shall love God, and adhere to God, and the more surely shall we finally reach God."

The words of the saintly priest completed the work that the letter of Lily had commenced. The stranger knelt by the corpse and was calm, if not happy. His thoughts had taken a different turn, he no longer wished for death in order to join his wife and child, but he was content to live, to carry out her last dying wishes, and by the performance of this good work, to testify his gratitude to God for the happy entrance of his beloved child into Heaven.

His friends asked him if he would not now return home.

He answered in the affirmative, but begged

to be allowed a few moments longer to pay another visit to the church.

When he had done this he got into the carriage, and they soon reached Portland Place. He stepped out and went upstairs to his apartment, where he remained during the rest of the day. No one attempted to intrude on his privacy, every one felt that a period of solitude and quiet must be necessary for him.

The next day, however, he came among them as usual, but was totally silent with regard to the past, and, in fact, seemed absorbed in thought, unable to join much in general conversation.

The funeral of Lily took place in the middle of the following week, and on the previous evening her coffin was carried to the convent church, and placed outside the altar-rails in front of the sanctuary.

A beautiful wreath of white roses and lilies was placed on the coffin, and her sorrowing father knelt at the side. Near to him knelt one whose grief, if not as great, was at least far more demonstrative, and that one was poor old Biddy, whose appearance there surprised every one.

Although still ill, and very weak, she had begged so earnestly to be allowed to go to see the last of her sweet "colleen," as she still called Lily, that the good ladies of Portland Place sent their carriage in the morning to convey her to the convent church.

The ceremony was performed in a reverential and imposing manner, and the stranger had made all the necessary arrangements for the remains of his child to be conveyed for interment to his family vault, at his castle in Scotland, where it would lie underneath the church. He did not, however, accompany the funeral to Scotland, but determined to stay a few days longer in London with his friends in Portland Place.

He wished to settle something with regard to the future maintenance of poor old Biddy, as he was quite determined she should never again feel the want of anything. His idea was to place her in a comfortable alms-house near his dwelling in Scotland, where each inmate had two nice rooms (a bedroom and sitting-room), besides a small kitchen and outhouse. But when he proposed this to Biddy, she refused his offer with many thanks, saying that she had been accustomed to sell fruit in the streets for so many years, that she should feel lonesome, with nothing to do in a strange place.

"No, if his honour would give her a stock of apples and fruit she could return to her stall when well enough, and she should then bless him, and be quite happy; at least as happy as she could be now that she had lost her 'sweet colleen.'"

The stranger agreed to everything she wished, and she called down the blessing of God upon him when he left her poor dwelling.

He was somewhat more cheerful that day at dinner in Portland Place, and in the evening addressed the master of the house and his family in these words—

"Until the present moment, my good friends, I have been totally unable to speak to you of those events in my past life which must still appear to you so mysterious, and which you naturally desire to have explained. You are, of course, at a loss to know how it was that I so totally lost sight of my beloved wife and child. It is rather a long tale, and a painful one, but you shall hear all."

"Oh! my dear sir," exclaimed the amiable

mistress of the house, "do not speak of anything if it gives you pain to do so,—some other day when you feel stronger will be the same to us."

It must be owned that the kind lady did not quite mean what she said, for she was most anxious to hear the explanation of the mystery, and the rest of the company were almost more so,—so anxious, indeed, that not one of them echoed her polite and unselfish speech, but they left the stranger to imagine (if he pleased) that they were all of the same opinion.

He, however, merely bowed in thanks, and said—

"If I do feel some pain in speaking of the past, it matters not, I deserve that pain and much more. I give you free leave to tell my history to any one you please; it may be beneficial to many, as it demonstrates clearly the miserable consequences of concealment. Secrecy may sometimes be so necessary as to render it praiseworthy, instead of wrong, but in the majority of cases you may be certain that where secrecy and dissimulation are required, there is something wrong in the matter. You will probably think that I had legitimate reason for concealing the fact I am about to narrate, but, for all that, it produced much misery; my fault was, doing a thing merely to please myself, which it was necessary to conceal. My wife frequently said to me with a sigh—

"'Oh, what a tangled web we weave,
When first we practise to deceive.'

"But now, I will commence my history without any more delay."

Every face in the company was turned towards the stranger with smiling eagerness, and he began his tale as follows.

CHAPTER XIX.

THE HISTORY OF THE STRANGER.

YOU all know, I believe, that I am Scotch, and that my family is very ancient. My father was proud of his ancestors, and delighted in nothing so much as recounting the many deeds of valour they had performed, during the constant bloody wars which raged between the English and Scotch before the two kingdoms were united into one.

My father was an upright character, but his many good qualities were totally obscured by excessive rigidity in all things connected with religion. He was feared by many, and loved by few; for in carrying out his own religious views he seemed quite to forget the great law of universal charity. He never reflected that, as he claimed religious liberty for himself, he ought to give the same to others, but, on the contrary, he even refused to associate with any person who did not hold his views. My mother adopted most of his religious tenets, and I fancy carried them even farther than he did himself, as is usually the case with ladies, but she was a thoroughly good and conscientious person.

It was the earnest desire of both my parents to instil their own principles into my young mind with the earliest dawn of reason, but strange to say, their efforts had the reverse effect from that intended; for, even as a boy, I was unusually careless and idle with regard to such matters. I perfectly detested the dry services and long sermons I was forced to attend, and I determined in my own mind that as soon as I was a man, and able to act as I pleased, I would throw off everything in the shape of religion.

I acted up to my determination, and as soon as possible gave up everything, proclaimed myself a free-thinker, and never went near a church or chapel of any denomination.

My dear mother mourned over my lax principles even more than my father, as her religious feelings were most sincere. It is true that she carried them out too austerely, and was (probably unknown to herself) filled with self-sufficiency, and, therefore, harsh in judging others.

I well remember overhearing a conversation between my mother and an old man (a retainer of the family) on the subject. She spoke of my irreligious behaviour, and lamented it with heartfelt grief, but he replied solemnly—

"If you draw the string of a bow too tight, it breaks in the end ; you drew his string over-tight when he was only a lad, now it is broken, and it is a question whether it will ever be mended. But as he is in many ways a good young man, moral, kind-hearted, and charitable, we must hope for the best; he may return to God some day if you leave him alone, and say nothing."

My mother sighed, but did not reply. My father, too, mourned over my lax principles, but hoped that increasing years might, as he said, steady me down and bring me round after a time. He gave up speaking to me at all on such subjects, as I only laughed at everything he said ; and having considerable talent for argument, I easily silenced him even when truth was on his side. I had not the least bias in favour of Catholics, but sometimes to provoke him, when he was praising the purity of his own faith, I would exclaim—

"Well! if there is truth in any religion at all (which I more than doubt), it must be found among those Papists whom you abuse so constantly, as they alone can be traced up to the time of the apostles. But I believe in no religion at all, my religion is *honour*, which makes me above doing anything that I consider either wrong or dishonourable."

I said this without much reflection, because I was provoked with my father, and, in truth, I knew a trifle more about Catholics than he did, from conversations with a young friend of mine who had many relations of that creed, and I was aware that many of the absurdities with which they are taxed were false, but for all that I was fully determined in my own mind that whatever change I might make in the future, I never would enter such a Church as that of the Papists. I detested nothing so much as submission, and laughed at the very idea of having to believe any rubbish the Pope might order, as I fancied Catholics were obliged to do.

One of my great pastimes was fishing. I was enthusiastically fond of the sport, as also of shooting, and I often spent weeks and even months in fishing localities. Sometimes I got a lodging for the night in a farmhouse, but I more frequently slept in an open barn, or under a tree. I was young and strong; that life of liberty suited me, and the sight of the beauties of nature in the wild woods gave me intense delight. This, in fact, was the only thing which awakened any religious feelings in my soul,—it did occasionally force me to reflect for a moment on the possible end of my creation, and cause some misgivings in my mind, as to whether the mysterious Being who had called me into existence might not demand of me something more than frittering away my best years in vain amusements. I at times felt a blank in my heart and a longing for an undefined something.

One evening, after I had been fishing all day, a thick fog came on suddenly, the darkness became quickly so dense that I could scarcely see my own hand. I was almost a mile from the cottage where I intended to sleep, and my sole companion was a little black and tan terrier whom I called Mouse.

The darkness was so great that I doubt much whether I should have thought it possible to find this cottage had I not relied on the instinct of my dog. I felt certain that it would find its way back again, because when we left the cottage in the morning it was busily employed in attacking a great black cat, and although the sport was abandoned when I called, and the cat left in a tree, yet I felt certain that the spunky little fellow would, if incited, guide me even in the dark to that cottage, in hopes of another encounter with its adversary.

So I called Mouse, and tied a bit of string which I happened to have in my pocket round his neck, and said in a brisk tone, "Go, catch cat, good dog!"

The little fellow understood me at once, and set off quickly. I followed with the certainty of being guided through the dark wood. When we had traversed a certain distance, we came to an old bridge which it was necessary to cross. Mouse, of course, skipped over safely in a moment, but my weight was a different affair. The night was too dark for me to make choice of that part which was not rotten, it cracked, bent, and finally gave way, and I was precipitated from the bridge on to the stones in the water below. The water was not deep, and I should have had no difficulty in scrambling out, but unfortunately my leg was broken just below the instep. I could not stand, much less walk, and was obliged to sit as best I could upon a large stone which happened to be in the middle of the running stream. What was to be done? I could not walk at all, but how could I possibly sit all night in the water on that stone with my clothes wet through from having fallen into the stream? I should certainly die from such exposure, and as I knew there were no dwellings in the vicinity, there seemed no possible hope of any one hearing me, or passing near that locality in such weather and so late at night. I felt quite in despair, and I, who always spoke as if I had no fear of death, trembled at the idea of such a miserable and lonely end.

The little dog could not, of course, understand the reason of my stopping and sitting down in the middle of the stream; it commenced barking loudly to make me proceed quickly. I endeavoured to silence it, as the noise worried me, but my anger was useless,—the little beast would continue to yelp.

Suddenly, to my unspeakable relief, I distinguished the sound of carriage wheels at no great distance from the bridge, but I was so exhausted, and so near fainting from the severity of the pain consequent on my broken leg, that I had not sufficient strength to call out and beg for assistance.

My heart sank within me for a moment, as I fancied the sound seemed to get at a greater distance; I feared all hope was at an end, that the carriage had merely crossed the road and gone on. But such was not the case, for when I again listened attentively I felt certain that it was approaching, although the coachman was driving very slowly on account of the dense fog.

When the carriage reached the vicinity of the bridge the occupants were struck by hearing the barking of my dog. They were surprised at the unexpected sound so late at night in such an unfrequented part; they imagined at first that it must be some man or boy trying to catch rabbits, but a moment's reflection showed them that this was not likely, and that it was far more probable that some person had lost his way in the dark, and that the dog was barking at the wild birds. They then thought it possible that some one might be ill or in distress, and the old gentleman told his servant to take one of the lanthorns from the carriage and walk up to the place where the little dog was barking, to see if assistance of any kind was required.

The servant approached the bridge, and soon saw and heard from me what had happened. He returned immediately to the carriage and told the old gentleman, who was seated in it with his daughter, the state of the case: and they both got out instantly and came to my assistance.

The old gentleman helped his servant to carry me to the carriage, while his daughter arranged the cushions comfortably, and tied up my broken limb to the best of her power with the handkerchief.

The old gentleman did not look more than sixty years of age, although his hair was quite grey, but he seemed weak, for he tottered as he assisted his servant in carrying me to the carriage. He was not exactly handsome, but he had a benevolent countenance, and looked thoroughly straightforward.

His daughter was apparently not much above eighteen, tall, slight, and elegant in appearance.

I have rarely seen eyes to compare with hers for beauty; they were dark blue, with deeply fringed eyelashes both above and below; her hair dark brown; and her sylph-like form reminded me forcibly of a young and timid fawn.

Her natural shyness, however, soon vanished when there was necessity for action. She bandaged my broken leg carefully, and perceiving that I was almost fainting from the severe pain, put her smelling-bottle to my nose, and made a sign to her father to give me some wine from the flask they had in the carriage.

I was unable to speak, but I pressed the hand of the old gentleman, who smiled and said—

"Agnes will take care of you; she is a first-rate nurse, as I know from experience."

We were not very long in reaching their home —a small red brick house. I was carried into the parlour, placed on the sofa, and the doctor sent for. My little dog had followed me closely, and now sat by my side. The doctor quickly arrived and examined the broken limb; he said that much pain and discomfort had been saved by the careful tying up and bandaging of Miss D——. He soon did what more was required; and after exhorting me to patience and calmness, took his leave, promising to return and see me early on the following day.

I sent a note to my father the next morning, to inform him of my accident, and to beg him and my mother to come and see me.

They did so without delay, and I told them directly they arrived of the great kindness and attention that my host and young hostess had shown me. I requested my father to ask to see them at once, and to express the warm gratitude he and my mother must feel. But to my surprise and annoyance they both refused, and replied, that I could say what was necessary, and that they should speak to the doctor and make arrangements for my being removed as soon as possible in an invalid carriage. I was excessively provoked, and expressed my anger in no measured terms. My father left the room without deigning a reply, but my mother remained a few moments longer and whispered—

"Be not astonished, my son; you have unfortunately fallen into a viper's nest. Surely you have heard your father speak of the D—— family!"

I started, for I had indeed heard my father speak in terms of the most fearful hatred of that family; but with the usual perversity of human nature, I now felt quite pleased at having been, unknown to myself, thrown among them, and thought I should now discover what the cause of offence had been, for my father had always been so mysterious and silent on the subject.

I made up my mind to remain with Mr. and Miss D—— as long as possible, and I persuaded the doctor, who was my intimate friend, to say that it would be dangerous for me to be removed for some time, lest fever should come on. During the first week of my sojourn in that house neither my father or my mother came near the place, but the old gentleman and his daughter nursed me with the greatest care and attention. I found him to be a most agreeable companion, well read, with much knowledge of the world, and thoroughly good and upright. He referred once, and only once, in conversation to the deadly feud which existed between his family and the family of my father; he said, "that that enmity had been one of his greatest sorrows in life, that he had done his utmost, but in vain, to overcome the prejudice and hatred of my father for himself and all his family, but could never convince him that persons ought not to be held accountable for the misdeeds of their forefathers, more especially as there are usually faults on both sides in such cases. He hoped, however, that the enmity would not be carried on to the next generation, as he thanked God for giving him an opportunity of doing me a real service."

I thanked him for his kindness and courtesy, and answered, "that, so far from sharing the ill-feeling, I should do all in my power to destroy the feud, and to let love and friendship take the place of the deadly hatred that had hitherto existed."

He shook his head and said, "I fear your efforts will be vain, but, at least, I am consoled by the certainty that the enmity will cease with the life of your father."

As Mr. D—— and his daughter had very small means they kept only one servant of all work, consequently I saw Miss D—— constantly; she waited on me, and nursed me when I first came and required unremitting attention. I admired her beyond measure, and, in truth, Agnes was superior in mind and in personal attractions to any young lady I had ever seen before. But what particularly delighted me was the great love and respect she evinced for her father; his slightest wish was her law, and the affection she showed him was unbounded. I had but little love and reverence for my parents, I considered them narrow-minded individuals, and the rigidity of their religious principles worried me, and, as I said before, made me despise everything connected with piety. My host rarely spoke of religion, but I was delighted with the universal charity he displayed towards the members of every denomination; he seemed really to act upon the words of Scripture, "Have charity one for the other."

Time passed by more rapidly than I wished; a full week had elapsed since my accident, and my parents had only been once to see me. I felt annoyed at their conduct, and in no hurry to return home. I signified my wishes to the doctor, and he, when my parents sent to ask how soon I could be removed, answered at once that he would not be responsible for the risk of removing me so soon, for that, if my leg got shaken, as was probable in traversing the bad roads, they might make up their minds to see me lame for the rest of my days.

This alarmed them, as their love for me was in truth very great, and they resolved to come once more to visit me, that they might judge for themselves how I was progressing, but they refused to see either my host or hostess, which rudeness on their part annoyed me so excessively, that I requested them not to come any more if they intended to display such ingratitude towards persons who had shown me such unbounded kindness and hospitality, and, in fact, saved my life.

They left the room in great wrath, and I cared not a straw for their anger, as I felt I was right. I was determined that I would not continue the family feud, but that when I was quite well I would still keep up my friendship for the good old man and his daughter.

I kept my resolution, and after my return home went constantly to see my friends, but kept my visits a profound secret from my parents. I went out shooting and fishing even more frequently than in former days, and always managed not to find either game or fish near home. I almost invariably found it at so great a distance from home that it was impossible to return until very late in the evening, and I frequently remained away all night. I need not say that these nights, and a great part of the days, were spent in the house of my friend Mr. D—— and his amiable daughter.

I was always welcomed with a smile, and I grew daily more and more intimate with both. It was natural that my visits should give them pleasure, as they saw so few persons in that retired locality, and I found their society most agreeable.

After these lengthened expeditions I always took care to return home with a good bag, which accounted for my long absence. The contents were not always, it is true, the produce of my own exertions, but that mattered not, for I let my parents suppose that it was so, and they were satisfied.

A year and a half had elapsed since my accident, and I perceived with regret that there was a great change for the worse in the health of Mr. D——; he seemed, in fact, to be breaking up rapidly. His daughter became uneasy about him, although from being constantly at his side, she was not as forcibly struck by the alteration as I was. But what she did see and grieve over, was the failing in his mind, his memory was almost gone, he remembered events that had occurred in former years, and forgot what had happened a few hours before. He talked constantly, and in a most childish manner. Fortunately his weakness of mind was of a happy description; far from being querulous or discontented, he laughed like a child about every trifle, and joked on the most serious subjects.

Miss D—— endeavoured to the best of her power to conceal this increasing ailment from others, but the attempt was vain, he never seemed happy unless treated as a child. The doctor who attended him said that his brain was gradually softening, and that this would probably in a few months be succeeded by a stroke of paralysis; he added, that if this came on he would not last long, as his constitution was so enfeebled by the hardships he had undergone in youth.

Miss D—— told me all the doctor had said, when I called one evening, as she saw it was useless to hide her fears and grief any longer. I listened with the greatest attention and sympathy to all she said, and answered—

"I have, indeed, remarked the change of

which you speak for some time, although I hope that he will not get worse as rapidly as the doctor predicts; they are so often wrong in their suppositions. However, your poor father is not young, and from what he has said to me I fancy his constitution was much tried in youth; therefore this break-up, although it seems to come suddenly upon us, is merely in the course of nature, but there are many other things to be thought of. Have you (if I may presume to ask), my dear Miss D——, considered what you shall yourself do when your father is taken from us."

"Oh yes, indeed I have; in fact, I have little, I may say, no choice. I have but one relation in the world—Aunt Sarah, usually called Aunt Sal, an old maiden sister of my mother, who lives in North Wales. I must go to her, for I shall be totally without means."

"Do you love this Aunt Sal?"

"Not in the least."

"Does Aunt Sal love you?"

"On the contrary, she dislikes me; because, when I was about ten years old, I pushed one of her pet cats into a washing-tub. She said she would never forgive me, but I suppose she would not now turn me out of her house in my distress, as I shall have no home."

"Do you expect to be happy with this eccentric old Aunt Sal?"

"No, on the contrary, I expect to be most uncomfortable; but remain with her I must, if she will allow me, until I can meet with a situation as governess in some family. I shall probably do this without much difficulty, as my dear father has educated me with such care, and I should try to go abroad."

"And we shall then, probably, never meet again," I answered in a low tone.

Miss D—— started, the colour left her face, and despite all efforts to control her feelings, tears came in torrents from her eyes, and she hid her face in her handkerchief.

Those tears told a tale that went to my heart. She had not shed a tear even when she spoke of the illness of her dear father, she had not shed a tear when speaking of her probable trials with Aunt Sal, or even at the idea of gaining her livelihood as a governess, but she wept at the idea of our never meeting again. She must love me, I mentally ejaculated; she must love me as devotedly as I love her. Yes, those tears spoke volumes to my heart; my resolution was instantly taken. I determined to marry her if she would accept me, to brave the anger of my father and mother, to marry her, despite the almost certainty of being disinherited, and to act in the matter at once. I put my hand on the small white hand which was on the table, and said—

"I do not ask you to speak, Miss D——; you are, I know, too much agitated to do so; but if, as I fondly hope, you love me as I love you, press my hand: I shall be content."

My pressure was returned gently,—oh, so gently! almost imperceptibly; and then, as if alarmed at what she had done, the hand was withdrawn quickly. But I was satisfied, and said tenderly—

"It is enough, leave the rest to me; I will soon arrange all."

"But your father, what will he say?"

"He must know nothing for the present, but after a little time I will ask his consent. Now I must take time to consider what is best to be done, and to-morrow I will return and let you know all I have arranged."

"Shall we try whether my dear father can

understand the matter sufficiently to give his consent?"

"We can make the attempt, if you please; but I fear he will understand nothing."

I approached the old man, roused him, and said—

"My good friend, will you give Agnes to me?"

He looked up cheerfully, almost as in former days, and answered courteously—

"By all means, my good sir; take her, and use her as long as you please, but return her when you have quite finished."

Miss D—— looked at me with a melancholy smile, for we both saw that he understood nothing, and only thought I wished to borrow a book, or something of the kind. It was useless to say more, therefore I left the house.

I returned the next morning according to promise, and was met at the door by Agnes, who told me, with consternation depicted on every feature, that the fears of the medical men had been too well-founded, for that her dear father had been seized with paralysis during the night, and now lay totally unconscious. I accompanied her instantly to his room, and saw at a glance that the end was fast approaching, and the doctor, when he arrived, confirmed our worst fears. I therefore said to Agnes, as I now ventured to call her—

"We must act promptly, there is no time to be lost, we must be married, and that without delay."

"But how can that be?" said Agnes in a trembling voice; "you have not yet asked the consent of your father; he may refuse, and what shall we do then?"

"Listen to me, dear Agnes, and do as I wish, for great prudence is necessary. If I asked my father's consent now, without having had time to prepare his mind, he would very likely refuse at once, and put us in an awkward dilemma; for we should not like to be married if he had decidedly said 'No.' I wish I had asked him about it before this, but I had no idea of your father's health breaking up so quickly. As things are we have no choice, we must get the marriage ceremony performed as soon as possible. I will get a special license, and if I have that, of course, any priest will marry us at once, as I am of age, and consequently my own master, and your father can neither give or refuse his consent, as he is childish. We need enter into no particulars, and your father's illness gives reason enough for all being done privately. Your old servant and a farmer whom I have known many years must be the witnesses, as their love for us will make them keep the matter secret. A friend of mine, to whom I have confided everything, will likewise in all probability be present, so hold yourself in readiness, dear Agnes, for to-morrow morning."

She looked at me with astonishment and dismay, and exclaimed in an imploring tone—

"Oh no, no indeed, indeed it must not be so, we cannot be married thus; there will be no blessing on such a clandestine marriage."

"But, dearest love, we cannot do otherwise; we have no choice; you know the immense importance of keeping the whole matter secret for the present. In a month or so I shall reveal everything to my father and mother, they will see that what is done cannot be undone, they will show a little displeasure for a time perhaps, but I shall soon put all that right, and when they know you they will say

I was quite justified in acting for myself; and then, Agnes, will come the joyful day for taking you to my ancestral home, for my father and mother to receive you into their arms."

"Ah! that will never, never be, I fear!"

"Then, you do not love me, Agnes. If you did love me, you would be willing to run some little risk for my sake."

"Oh! but, indeed, I love you too well, too well, alas! for our happiness."

"Then show your love, Agnes, by yielding your opinion. You are but a woman, and cannot take the enlarged view any sensible man would. I only ask you to keep the marriage concealed for a time, for a short time."

"But even that is wrong, and a wrong thing ought not to be done for the chance of future good."

"You are quite mistaken, dearest love; there is nothing really wrong in this. I am of age, and have the right to marry if I please; it is not as if my father would have any real reason for refusing his consent, only it does not do to run risks."

Agnes did not reply, but looked at me sadly,

she could not agree in my view of the case, and yet she feared to oppose me. She was not aware of my being an Atheist, and thought I would not do anything wrong. I continued gently—

"When we are married I shall have no difficulty in carrying out my plan, which I will now explain to you. It is this: that directly the funeral of your poor father is over, and his few legal affairs settled, you leave this place accompanied by your old servant, to whom everything must be confided. The few friends whom you leave behind will suppose (and you must not undeceive them), that you are going to North Wales, as you intended, to live with your Aunt Sarah. But instead of that, the conveyance which I shall provide for you will take you to the Highlands, where I have a small property, which was given to me by my father when I came of age. A good house stands on it, which I live in whenever I go there for shooting or fishing, and when you are no longer in this part of the country I shall go there very frequently. I shall furnish the house comfortably, and establish you there with your old servant. No suspicion will, of course, excited by my spending weeks, or even months, with you there, as I have done this at times ever since my father gave me the property as a shooting-box."

"But all this is such deception, such an underhand proceeding," exclaimed Agnes in a desponding tone; "and my dear father had such a horror of secret transactions, of mysteries. He always said that no good ever came of acts which required concealment, that there was almost always something wrong in the sight of God. And what shall we have to live upon? I know that the allowance your father makes you is so very small."

"I have, besides the allowance of my father, £1000, which was left to me by my godmother. It is at present invested, but the interest I receive is so small, that I intend to put it out in something more lucrative which a friend has told me of. You will have about £25 a year from your father when he dies, therefore, we shall manage pretty comfortably until I consider it prudent to inform my father of our marriage. I shall be able to supply you with both game and fish when I am with you, which will help you in household expenditure, and you will not be obliged to spend much on dress, as the only neighbours will be a lame old man and a blind old woman."

"But how long do you think it will be before you are able to declare our marriage, for there is something so dreadful in all this secrecy,—troubles always come from underhand transactions."

"It is impossible to name a time for declaring our marriage, and we have no alternative but concealment, in this case, dear Agnes, so set your mind at ease, and rest assured that everything shall be told to my father and mother as soon as possible; it would be complete ruin to do so now."

Unwillingly and sorrowfully did Agnes at last consent to carry out my arrangements, and it pained and almost provoked me to see that her heart was heavy and filled with misgivings as to the future.

I, however, considered the line of conduct I was pursuing as being perfectly necessary, and I certainly was troubled with no scruples in the business; the only thought which gave me a moment's uneasiness was the great reluctance of Agnes, but that could not be changed, so I said no more on the matter.

x

All was carried out as I had planned. We were married, after which I returned home for a time, after having made Agnes promise to write to me every day.

Two days after my departure I received a few hurried lines, to say that her father was much worse, and that if I wished to see him once more before death I must come without delay. I did so, and when I arrived was taken instantly to the bedroom of the invalid.

At that moment Agnes was bending over her poor father, trying to persuade him to take a little food, which he refused, and I made her a sign not to press him any more, as I perceived at once that he was dying, and had no longer the power to swallow.

We stood together, looking at the dying countenance and inanimate form of the good old man, when suddenly his eyes resumed that bright expression which had pleased me so much when I first saw him, and I perceived that reason was returned, although probably for only a few moments before death, but he knew us both, he seized a hand of each convulsively, pressed them together in his own two, and said—

"May God bless and preserve you both." He then looked at me and said, " Take care of her."

These were his last words, the death-rattle followed immediately, and his soul had taken flight.

We remained for some moments with our hands locked together in his, and it was a consolation to persuade ourselves that he had in a certain degree ratified and blest our union.

The funeral took place before the end of the week. It was as simple as possible, and very few persons attended as he had scarcely any friends in that part of the world.

The few friends who did come took it for granted that Agnes was going to live with her Aunt Sarah, therefore we had no difficulty; on that head silence was sufficient as to future plans.

The day after the funeral Agnes left the house with her old servant; they soon rejoined me in the Highlands, where I had preceded them, and as it was the season for shooting grouse I was able to remain with her nearly a month.

Ever after that my time was spent alternately with my parents and my wife, and at the end of the first year she presented me with an infant, the sweet Lily whose death we now mourn.

The birth of my child was a blissful moment for both of us; she looked at it with fond love, and I regarded it with delight, because I felt how much more happy Agnes would now be with something to occupy her mind during my unavoidable absences. She would have less time to think, and to mourn over what she called the duplicity of our conduct.

CHAPTER XX.

CONTINUATION OF THE HISTORY OF THE STRANGER.

YEARS slipped by, my child was almost six years of age, and there was no change in our position, my parents were still unaware of the secret marriage. I had never mustered courage to tell them of it; I had deferred the disclosure from month to month, always thinking I should find a more favourable moment, and when such a long time had passed I felt that the fact of my having kept everything thus concealed would make my father far more indignant than if I had told him the truth openly and at once.

Nevertheless, I still kept up a weakly-formed intention of telling him the truth in the end, but suddenly even this wavering intention was dashed to the ground by a chance conversation with my father, in which from something he said I understood him to infer that he had made a vow never to give his consent to any one belonging to him marrying into the D—— family, and I felt certain that if he had taken this oath no power in heaven or on earth, or entreaties on my part, would prevent his keeping his vow strictly. If he refused his consent he would, likewise, no doubt, seal his decision by cutting me off with a penny, for I believed all he possessed to be entirely in his own power, that he could make me either a rich man or a beggar. The latter was not even to be thought of, therefore I told Agnes the state of the case, and she was obliged to relinquish all hope of ever seeing our marriage acknowledged.

In the first years of my married life I did not suffer much inconvenience from poverty, as I had a certain sum in hand, therefore I was happy, notwithstanding occasional anxiety, for I found the character of my wife even superior to what I had imagined; but later I embarked my one thousand pounds in a large business which, although said to be no speculation, unfortunately turned out to be so.

This business was the working of some coal

and iron mines in Maryland. I was told that I should receive nine or ten per cent. for my money, therefore, in an unlucky hour, I sent it out.

The first outlay in commencing these works was so much larger than was anticipated, that the subscribers received no interest at all for their money, and I, having so little besides, found the greatest difficulty in making ends meet at all. I had no religious feelings to support me, and my secret was a constant weight on my mind. I was in perpetual fear of some chance circumstance divulging it. Agnes, on the contrary, had had true piety instilled into her mind from the earliest dawn of reason; and even I, strange to say, admired her devotion. I felt that it increased the charms of her character, and I decided in my own mind that although there was nothing *real* in religion itself, yet that it was good for women; as it certainly gave a softness of manner which rendered them more lovable. I could not conceal from myself that it was religion alone which rendered Agnes so much more patient and forbearing than myself, for she had much to try her. Although, in truth, I loved her devotedly, yet my troubles and anxieties rendered me irritable, and this, of course, made her feel all much more. She loved me, and felt for me in my uncomfortable position, but she was ever gentle, ever patient, and so forgiving, too. She had much, very much, to try her, for she suffered equally, and, in fact, more than myself, from our want of means; and my irritability gave her constant pain, besides feeling all the misery of her position as an unacknowledged wife.

I ought, indeed, to have comforted and supported instead of worrying her, as I often did. It is true that at times I was filled with remorse, and tried my best by kindness and attention to render her happy, and these were the only bright moments in her existence, but they passed rapidly like gleams of sunshine.

I allowed her to educate our child as she pleased. I was even anxious for it to be pious and good as she was herself. I allowed this because the child was a girl; had it been a boy, I should have insisted on what I considered a more manly and noble education. Religion would have been put on one side altogether, as only calculated for women and weak minds. I deluded myself into the idea that I neither feared

The History of the Stranger. 329

anything in this world nor in the next, and I should have educated a son with my own notions.

But although I tried to fancy that I believed nothing, yet there were moments when I could not banish doubt,—doubt as to whether, after all, I was not a fool, and those persons wise, who, like my wife, considered the things of this world merely as a preparation for something that was never to end, but which we should not comprehend until called from this life.

The moments when these doubts tormented me most was usually after sitting by the side of my dear gentle wife, when she instructed little Lily. I could not help being touched, and I hearkened with the greatest pleasure to all she said,—her religious ideas were so different from those of my stern parents. Tears often filled my eyes when she recounted pious tales, and the beautiful legends of the saints and angels in order to please and to amuse her child. I fancied I only listened in order to satisfy little Lily, as she sat on her mother's knee, smiling first at "Pappy," then at "Mammy."

But the undoubting faith of Agnes, and the comfort she found in her belief, made a greater impression on my heart than I was aware of at the time, and this impression produced fruit in after years, thanks be to God !

Two more years passed by, Lily was almost seven. She was a beautiful and engaging child, with her mother's fine eyes, good features, an d brilliant expression.

She was precocious in some ways from living constantly with her mother, but she was at the same time unusually simple in her ideas, from the fact of never associating with children older than herself, or, in fact, with any children at all, her only amusements being found in looking after cats, birds, and other pet animals. We took the precaution of concealing our family name, and forbade the old servant telling her anything concerning her relations. This secrecy seemed in truth an unnecessary precaution, as the child never saw any one to whom she could talk, but when persons have something to conceal they never think they can be sufficiently careful.

By degrees my affairs went on from bad to worse. I had been some years without receiving a penny of interest from America, and I was compelled to borrow money to make ends meet at all. This made me wretched, but I could not let my wife and child starve. The health of my father was good; therefore I had not even the poor consolation of thinking that I should before long come into possession of his estate. His health was, in fact, better than my own, for anxiety and worry had injured my naturally strong constitution.

I consulted my friend the doctor, and he, to my great joy, recommended change of air and scene. He told my father that unless something was done for me immediately, he would not answer for the consequences.

My father acceded at once to the proposal of the doctor, and declared himself ready to pay the expense of the journey, wherever it might be. I said I had no fancy for travelling anywhere in Europe, that I should like to try the New World. I had heard much of the magnificent scenery in some parts of the Alleghany mountains in Maryland, and should like to go there.

My father marvelled at my choice, as he had felt certain I should prefer Italy or France, on account of all that is to be seen in those countries, in the way of art and science, calculated to interest and improve me, whereas, in the mountains of Maryland, I should only see beauties on a larger scale than in the mountains of Scotland.

My poor father little thought that my one idea in wishing to travel in Maryland was the hope of discovering, during my visit there, whether there was any chance of my ever receiving any interest for the money I had sent out, or whether it was irretrievably lost.

One concealment is certain to cause many others, and now I had no choice. I was compelled to acts of duplicity to ensure secrecy. I felt humbled at my position, and bitterly lamented my first false step in the beginning, when I first deceived and visited Agnes and her father. I felt like a snowball which continues to roll on, on, constantly augmenting in size, and I trembled as I beheld the increasing mass of duplicity in which I was involved,—I trembled, but did not dare take the only step which could free me, lest it should involve myself, wife, and child in utter ruin; I bowed down my head in despair, misery, and shame.

And now, my good friends, said the stranger, looking at the deeply-interested group around him, you must allow me to pause, and, in fact,

to defer the rest of my melancholy tale until
to-morrow; what follows is so sad that I have
not strength to speak of it at present, and so,
good-night.

CHAPTER XXI.

THE VOYAGE OUT.

ON the following day the stranger recommenced his sad narrative in these words:—

I left my beloved wife and child with a heavy heart, but as she saw clearly that the step was necessary, that it was, in fact, the only chance of recovering anything, she made no opposition to my departure, and I went to Southampton to embark by a large steamer of the Bremen line, which always touched there to take up passengers.

As I was fond of the sea I quite enjoyed the idea of being out a fortnight, which is the usual time of the passage from Southampton to Baltimore. The ship was not overcrowded, therefore I had the comfort of a cabin to myself.

There were many pleasant English, American, and German passengers on board, whose society I enjoyed much, but the person who took my fancy above all the others, was a venerable grey-headed priest, who was on his way back to his mission in America after a visit to some relations who lived in the vicinity of Bremen, whom he had not seen for many years before. His name was Father Ignatius, he was of German origin, but had emigrated to America when he was first ordained priest. He spoke English perfectly, and could therefore converse in it on any subject. His constant kindness and amiability made him a general favourite with the passengers, but the universal knowledge he possessed made me seek his society, and we frequently sat together in the evening when all was still around us, and conversed for hours.

From the first day I made his acquaintance I was struck by the devout expression of his countenance. I felt drawn towards him, while he, on his part, seemed to take a particular fancy to me. He probably pitied me, as he was not long in discovering my infidel opinions. I, of course, was not aware of this, and naturally we like those who seem to take an interest in our concerns.

He quite won my confidence, and I told him the reasons which had decided me to undertake the long voyage to America. He gave me much valuable advice, but said I had made choice of an unfortunate moment for my visit to that country, as it was now torn to pieces and in a state of the greatest misery, from the effects of the fearful intestine war which was raging between the Northern and Southern powers.

Like other civil wars it was terrible beyond description. The nearest relatives took different sides, according to their individual interests; brothers were fighting against brothers, sons against their father, uncles and nephews against one another, battles and destruction were going on—on all sides. Travelling was most dangerous, and in order to reach that part of Maryland where the coal and iron mines in question lay, I should have to traverse the very midst of the theatre of war. He almost advised me to defer my visit for a time, but I would not hear of this, because, in the first place, I thought I should rather enjoy the excitement of seeing a little of the war of which I had heard so much, and secondly, my need of money was so great that I was ready to take any amount of trouble, and even to run some risk in the hope of obtaining the interest due from what I had embarked in the Maryland coal and iron mines.

One evening I asked him a few questions concerning his own life, and he gave me a slight sketch of the principal events. There was little variety, it is true, but the details he gave me of all that he himself and his fellow priests underwent, when his mission at St. Louis' was visited by that terrible scourge the small-pox, interested me much.

He told me how the day was spent in going about comforting the sick, and administering the last sacraments to the dying. Scarcely a night had passed without their being called up two or three times to fresh cases. He told me how one of his fellow-labourers, quite a young priest, caught the fatal disease from one whom he attended, and died at the end of two days. He himself and the other priest escaped the infectious disease, but were so exhausted in the end by their labours, as to be obliged to give up all missionary work for a time, in order to recruit their health.

"My good sir," I exclaimed in astonishment, "is it possible that such risk, such killing labour, can pay in the end?"

"Pay! what do you mean?"

"I mean, does all this exertion, risk, and labour, bring you that pleasure, procure you that happiness, which is the only thing worth seeking in this world? but which I candidly own, I have always sought, and never yet found."

"It doubtless gives a feeling of calm and happiness, but that happiness, that calm, springs from a source which you, I fear, cannot comprehend."

"And why should I not comprehend it?"

"Because this feeling of calm and happiness, in the midst of the greatest sufferings and privations, comes only from the love of God, and the wish to please Him by devoting our lives, our health, and every talent we may possess to the service of our fellow-creatures, for the simple reason that our Lord expressly says that what we do for them we do for Him."

"Bah! yes, you are right, I could find no happiness in this, for I neither believe in a God, nor in a hereafter."

"And who gives you the faculty of thinking at all about it? and who gives you the power of seeing, hearing, and understanding?"

"Oh! these things come naturally, I can't tell how."

"What do you mean by 'come naturally'? Why have you these faculties more than a magnificent oak? It is alive like you."

"Oh yes, but that is only a tree; of course, it cannot hear, and see, and speak."

"Why not? why do these things not come naturally to the tree as well as to you?"

"Oh! because, because"——

I paused, fairly puzzled what to answer, and Father Ignatius continued in an impressive tone, such as I had never before heard him assume—

"Who is it, I ask you, young man, who gives you all these powers, and does not give the same to the trees, and gives you the faculty of reason (which you so sadly abuse), and does not give it to the brutes around you? And who is it that could take away your life, and all your gifts, at once? You have knowledge enough of medicine to be aware, that the slightest deviation in the circulation of the blood from the right course in its passage from the heart to the brain would cause instant death,—human means, you know, would be totally unavailing to prevent this. Why have you been placed in this world at all? and why have you been thus carefully preserved for so many years, if not, by the mercy of God, in order to give you the chance of opening your eyes to the truth, that in the bright and unexpected light which would then flash upon you, you might for ever renounce these mad and foolish theories, and bow down your proud head in humble submission to your Creator, and endeavour to fulfil the end for which He created you? You cannot, I am certain, believe in your heart the foolish infidel opinions you allow your tongue so constantly to utter; but you silence reason, you will not reflect, because, if you did, you know full well that you would feel nothing save remorse and wretchedness, and therefore you stifle every doubt that arises in your mind. But mark my words, young man, you were put into this world to serve and glorify your Maker, and if you continue thus to spurn Him, and mock Him, and deny Him, you will one day be summoned out of this life when you least expect it, and when you stand before your Judge, you will be condemned for eternity to that dreadful abode where there shall be 'weeping and gnashing of teeth,' because you would not believe."

Sceptic as I was, his words, which seemed as if inspired, filled me with a terror that I could not shake off. I tried to smile and treat his words as a mere jest, but it was in vain, something seemed to choke my utterance. I arose hurriedly, and faltered out—

"Good-night, it is getting late."

Father Ignatius looked at me, his expression was kind and compassionate in the extreme, and he said in a low but earnest voice—

"Good-night, and may the God of mercy have compassion on you, and open your eyes, that you may save that precious soul which was redeemed by His blood."

I retired to my small cabin, with the intention of going to bed and trying to forget in sleep all these unpleasant ideas, but although I was soon comfortably ensconced between my blankets, yet I could not sleep, I could not rest. If I dozed for a few moments the words of Father Ignatius seemed to resound in my ears like a death knell. The heat was excessive, I threw off my covering, but to sleep was impossible. There had been a dead calm all day, with a hot sun, and not even a breath of air sprang up as usual at sunset. I felt fevered, oppressed, wretched, filled with remorse and black despair. Once I jumped out of bed and actually seized my razor with the full intention of putting an end to my life and misery at once, but the words of Father Ignatius reverberated in my soul, "You will be condemned for eternity to that dread abode where there is weeping and gnashing of teeth."

I tossed down my razor, and threw myself frantically on the bed, but did not remain there long, I again stood trembling by the side of the berth.

A momentary calm came over my mind, although my doubts, my sceptical feelings, stood as a host before me, but a sudden impulse seized me, which I seemed not able to resist. I threw myself on my knees and ejaculated in imploring accents—

"If there is a God, I adjure, I beseech Him to manifest Himself to me."

The words were scarce out of my mouth, when such a flash of lightning passed through the cabin as almost blinded me, and it was followed instantaneously by a clap of thunder, which shook the ship as if a thousand cannons had been levelled against her. The shock threw me on the floor, and there I remained I know not how long, but the work of God was done; with that flash of lightning the darkness of my mind was dispelled, doubt had vanished, faith had taken the place of infidelity. Prostrate as I was on the floor I made the first act of faith I had ever made in my life, and I promised God that I would henceforth try to serve Him so faithfully as to make up, as far as was in my power, for my many years of neglect.* I arose from my knees a changed man, I threw a cloak over my shoulders, left my cabin and directed my steps to the berth of Father Ignatius. His door was partly open on account of the heat; he was not in bed, the fearful flash of lightning and clap of thunder had roused him too, but he was kneeling tranquilly and peacefully before the little crucifix he always carried about with him.

He started when he saw my pale face and agitated countenance, and exclaimed—

"My good sir, what is the matter? are you alarmed at this fearful thunderstorm? come in here, and remain with me until it has passed

* A fact, excepting that he was in a railway carriage.

over." But to his surprise I approached, cast myself at his feet, and ejaculated in broken accents—

"Reconcile me to God, Father; reconcile me to God, for He has manifested Himself to me, I am no longer an infidel. Speak, say what I must do."

Never shall I forget the expression of joy which lighted up the face of Father Ignatius, as he looked up to heaven and thanked God most fervently for the mercy He had shown me. He took my hand, pressed it warmly, and said— "Be calm, my son; say this one prayer with me, and then take that repose which you so greatly need."

The prayer he recited was short, but it was a fervent act of contrition for the many sins of my past life, and a promise, on my part, by the grace of God, to serve Him faithfully in future, and begging Him to fill my heart with His love. I added, myself, a petition that was heard, and granted so fully, that I should have trembled as I made it if I had known what it entailed. This petition was, that God in His mercy would deign to send me temporal punishment in this world to expiate my many years of sinful infidelity.

Father Ignatius put his hand on my shoulder in a paternal manner, and said—

"My son, you perhaps know not what you ask, but that God whose grace has moved you to make this petition, will likewise grant you the grace and the strength to bear what is necessary to purify your soul. Now, go and lie down on your bed, and seek the repose you need."

I obeyed as a child would obey its mother. I had not been in bed many minutes, before I saw Father Ignatius enter my little cabin; he seated himself with his office-book in his hand, near my bed, and sat motionless, wrapped up in prayer. He afterwards told me that he was afraid of leaving me alone in such a state of excitement.

To my surprise I soon fell asleep, and slept until rather later than usual on the following morning. When I first awoke, my mind was in a state of confusion, and it was only by degrees that I was able to recall the events of the past night, but when at last I remembered everything clearly, there was still a feeling of calm and inexpressible peace in my mind. I arose from my bed, knelt on the floor, and for the first time since I was a boy at school, I bowed down my head and adored my Maker, and marvelled to think how for so many years I had doubted His existence; I say doubted, for although I had spoken and vaunted as if without doubt, yet there always seemed to be a small voice resounding in my soul, whispering, "Thou fool, thou fool."

Father Ignatius had been on deck many hours, he received me with paternal kindness, and we conversed on various interesting subjects, but he would not allow me to refer to the events of the past night, he wished my mind to become thoroughly calm before I acted. When I said—"Father, what am I to do now?" his reply always was, "Pray, that is sufficient for the present."

It was not until almost a week had passed since the wonderful event, that he allowed me to speak of my past life. I then told him everything connected with myself, my secret marriage, and my reasons for concealing it.

He listened attentively to all, he compassionated my painful position, but he most strongly advised me to brave the anger of my father, and to tell him everything. "Throw yourself on the generosity of your father, run any risk, rather than continue to lead such a life of duplicity, one concealment involves others, as you have found by experience. Let the first act of your return to God be, to accept the deep humiliation of confessing everything to your father. If he is high-minded, as your words lead me to suppose, you will not repent the act, even in a worldly point of view; but should he continue stern, and refuse to forgive, still you will feel that you have done what is right in the sight of God, and be able to offer up what you may have to suffer in expiation for the faults of so many years. Take courage, my good sir, do what is right, and do it without delay."

I was greatly moved by the words of Father Ignatius, and I promised to follow his advice, but I deferred, alas! the fulfilment of my promise until my return to England. Had I followed the path of duty at once, how much suffering might even then have been saved.

Father Ignatius told me that he must leave Baltimore directly we arrived, as his mission required his presence immediately, but that he would give me letters of introduction to the Archbishop of that city, who would instruct and give me all the assistance I required. I wrote a long letter to my wife before I left the ship, telling her everything that had occurred, and I posted it immediately on landing. I grieved much at having to say adieu to Father Ignatius, but he promised to write to me occasionally. He recommended me to go to the Mount Vernon Hotel (a large family hotel in Monument Street), as many persons from the country took apartments there for the winter months. Each person had, if they wished it, a good-sized sitting room, besides their bedroom, but all took their meals in the large public room, which was furnished with small tables, where each could have what he pleased, and need not associate with any one else.

I called on the Archbishop the day after we reached Baltimore, and as I had sent him Father Ignatius' letter on the previous evening, he received me with the greatest kindness.

He was a tall and portly-looking ecclesiastic, much beloved by his clergy, and highly respected by all who knew him, for his exemplary life. His talents were of the highest order, and he could converse on any subject. He gave me much good advice as to my future spiritual life, and I talked to him, likewise, about my temporal affairs, my reasons for coming out to America, and I asked if he had by chance heard of the Maryland coal and iron speculation. He answered that such matters were not exactly in his line, and that he knew little or nothing of the affair in question. He, however, promised to give me an introduction to a gentleman who resided in the vicinity of the mines, who, in fact, was one of the original managers of the business, and who would, he was certain, give me all the information in his power.

The gentleman in question belonged to a good old English family. He came over to America when quite a youth, and settled in Maryland, being one of the persons sent out by the subscribers to watch over their interests in conjunction with the directors of the mines. He was expected at the hotel in the course of the week, and when he arrived the good archbishop sent a note to request to see him, in order that he might have the pleasure of introducing an Englishman who was desirous of making his acquaintance.

Mr. Crighton called at the time named by

the archbishop, and I was at once introduced to him. I have rarely met a more prepossessing person, and the kind manner in which he assured me that he should have the greatest pleasure in giving me all the information in his power, quite gained my heart in this first interview; and, I must add, that a nearer acquaintance increased my esteem for his character. I have seldom seen a more straightforward and high-minded individual.

However, the account he gave me of the prospects of the coal and iron company in the mountains, was anything but cheering. He said that they had long ceased working the iron, and that the furnaces were out of blast. Coal was the only commodity that returned any interest for the money expended, and this part of the concern was principally in the hands of the American subscribers, who, being on the spot, looked after the money matters, and would not be likely to allow much to leave the country for England.

Mr. Crighton kindly asked me before he left, to come and spend a few weeks with himself and his wife at his residence in the mountains, as he lived within half a mile of the iron and coal mines. I accepted this invitation most thankfully, and we agreed that I should go to him in about a fortnight, as I wished, for many reasons, to spend that time in Baltimore. I had, whilst on board the steamer, written a long letter to my dear wife, which I had sent by a ship which was just starting when we reached Baltimore. I told her every particular of the wonderful event which had converted me, and enlightened my darkness, and I anticipated in my own mind the delight and happiness which would fill her heart on hearing such unexpected news, as my total want of religion had been the only bar to our felicity and complete union since we married. My wife received my letter in the course of ten days, and answered it instantly, in these words—

" DEAREST AND MOST BELOVED HUSBAND,— It is utterly impossible for me to describe the intense joy which inundated my heart when I read the letter I received from you to-day. I cannot say how often, or how fervently, I have implored Almighty God to grant this favour. I felt that no human arguments could shake your opinions, that nothing but a grace almost as great as that accorded to St. Paul would convert you. I implored God to bring about the work which no power of reasoning could effect, to change your heart Himself. I exclaimed in the fervour of my desire, 'Oh, my God, send something astounding, and if you grant me this, and I can know for certain that he is converted from infidelity, I will not repine if you think it good to take him out of this life, to deprive me of the only being (except my child) whom I love on earth,—no, far from repining, I will receive that affliction with resignation, and only rejoice and give thanks that my prayer for his return to you has been granted. I will submit without a murmur to the loss of all that is dear to me on earth, if I can only hope that his soul is safe, that he is striving to gain the happiness of heaven.'

"And now, beloved husband, now that God has in such a wonderful manner granted my prayer, I cannot command my feelings; my heart palpitates with terror at the thought, that as my petition has been granted, the exchange I offered may likewise have been accepted; that perhaps I shall never again behold your loved countenance, never again see you, my dearest spouse, my only support, whom I love better, far better than myself.

"You are now in the midst of a horrible war. You are an Englishman, it is true, and take no part on either side, but in civil war all laws of justice are put on one side, might takes the place of right. Take care of yourself, I implore you; do not run into needless danger. Think what I, what your child, would be if deprived of you, my husband, my protector, my sole tie on earth except my dear child! Do not remain longer than is quite necessary in America, but calm my fears by a speedy return.—Your devoted WIFE."

I received this letter before leaving Baltimore. I could not, of course, give up my promised visit to Mr. Crighton, but I wrote my wife a short letter, telling her that it was quite necessary for me to go into the mountains for a few weeks, but that I should then return home at once; therefore I entreated her to keep her mind calm and happy, as I would take the greatest care not to run into any danger. I heard afterwards that the ship in which I sent this letter was lost, consequently she never received it.

z

I left Baltimore for the residence of Mr. Crighton in the beginning of September. I only took my ticket as far as Cumberland (about two hundred miles), as he had kindly promised to meet me there, and drive me in his buggy the last ten miles of my journey, that I might be able to enjoy the beauty of the scenery of that part of the country. He kept his promise and was ready at the dépôt to greet me directly the train reached Cumberland.

The road was far more rough and hilly than any road I had ever traversed in England, but the horses were accustomed to the country, and the build of the Welmington buggy is so light that we passed over every impediment without danger, or even much discomfort, and in a very short time reached the residence of my friend,—a pretty, picturesque house, with a large and wide veranda round three sides of it. Most of the houses in America have verandas, not so much as a matter of ornament, as of necessity, for the heat of the sun is so great in the summer, as also the glare, that the shelter of a balcony is required to render the rooms habitable. When I arrived in the beginning of September the heat was much decreased, and the humming-birds, which go there occasionally, had ceased their visits, therefore I had not the pleasure of seeing one.

My friend's house was almost on the summit of a high hill which overlooks a deep valley, through which flows the river Potomac.

On the opposite side the eye can follow long ranges of the Alleghany mountains, and in this valley are situated the coal and iron mines in which I had unfortunately invested all my money. It was cheerful to see the railway cars passing swiftly along the lines of railway connected with the coal mines; they were numerous, and the black cars looked in the distance, as they glided quickly round the sides of the mountain, like so many black caterpillars crawling along; and all came to one terminus in the centre of the valley.

I spent almost a week with my friend and his amiable wife. I was enchanted with the wild scenery of the country, and I used to sit for hours with them under their large balcony, looking again and again at the ranges of mountains in the distance, and wishing to know their different names, that I might be able to recall them all vividly to my mind when I returned to England.

"Can you," I said one day, addressing my host, "can you tell me the name of each of these mountains? For instance, what is the name of the fine, large, thickly-wooded one in front of us?"

"That is Mount Savage, or Big Back-bone mountain. In olden times the early settlers called the Indians the savages, and as after a raid the Indians would always stop their retreat, and make fight against all pursuers on this mountain, the settlers called it the Savage mountain.

"The hill to the east of this valley is called Dan's mountain, because Dan, who was a son of Colonel Cussago, was killed on it. It formed the great mountain in front of Cussago town, which lay in the valley, and was the residence of Colonel Cussago of 'Logan fame,' and his family.

"The high mountain in the vicinity is called Will's mountain; it was so named after an Indian of that name, who was domesticated in the family of Colonel Cussago.

"This Indian was the last of the many who

inhabited this part of the country. He died in the woods while hunting, and at his own dying request was buried with his feet to the east, his dog across his feet, and his bow and arrows by his side, so that he might enter the happy hunt-grounds all prepared for the chase, and not be beholden to any one for food or clothing.

"But the most curious of all," said my host, "is the anecdote recounted concerning Negro mountain, that which you see about twenty miles west of Savage mountain. It was thus called after a favourite negro slave of that same Colonel Cussago, of the name of Numisus.

"This slave always accompanied the Colonel in his Indian campaigns, but on one occasion when desired to do so made answer—

"'Massa, I no wish to go, for I had a dream last night. I dreamed that you said we would go on one more expedition against the Indians, and we started with our pack on our backs, and our rifles in our hands. It was a beautiful morning, but all as we went up Jenning's run, and I heard the stream falling over the stones, as I had done many times before, it kept always saying as though in words, " Turn back,

Numisus, turn back," and the echoes replied, "Turn back, turn back." And as we turned through the birch wood the jay bird screeched out, over and over again, "Turn back, turn back." And when we stood on the summit of Savage mountain, the wind, sighing as it passed through the giant pines, whispered even more sorrowfully, "Turn back, turn back." But, massa, we went on, for Numisus would not leave his master, and we met the Indians at the crossing of the Gonghiohens, and we fought, and we pursued them. But, massa, I did not return, and when you reached the house of Cussago alone, I seemed to hear your sons ask you, "Where is Numisus?" and you replied, "The brave fellow sleeps at the foot of the Giant Hemlock, on the mountain beyond the little crossing, and in his memory it shall be called by us and by our children and children's children, "Negro Mountain."'

"'Fear not,' replied Colonel Cussago, 'fear not, these are mere old women's omens; come with me, and return again in glory to-morrow night.'

"Numisus yielded to the wishes of his master, and accompanied him in pursuit of the

Indians, but in the midst of the encounter which followed a gigantic Indian struck him with his tomahawk, and his master only arrived in time to save his scalp. He was buried where he fell; the mountain now bears his name, and his memory is still cherished in the family."

Mr. Crighton told me many other interesting facts about the surrounding country; however, I will narrate no more at present, but continue my own sad narration.

I spent upwards of a month with my kind friends, and saw everything worth going to in that part of the country. I ascertained beyond doubt that I could do nothing with regard to the money I had unfortunately risked, but leave it where it was, and hope for the best as to receiving interest in the future. My friend promised to do anything in his power to help me if opportunity offered (and he kept his word), therefore I determined to start for England as soon as possible, knowing how anxious my wife must be for my return.

I made a firm resolution to act openly, and directly I reached England tell my father at once, both of my secret marriage, and the change that had taken place in my religious opinions. I resolved to run any risk rather than conceal the smallest circumstance.

The war was still raging fearfully between the North and the South, therefore there was doubtless some risk in travelling at such a time; but I had no choice in the matter, I could not delay, and therefore fixed my day for starting.

I bade farewell to my kind host and hostess, promising to visit them again if it was ever in my power to do so, and the former agreed to write to me occasionally, and to give me news of the coal and iron mines.

CHAPTER XXII.

THE CAPTURE AND IMPRISONMENT.

THE train left the dépot (the term by which the station is designated) at eight o'clock in the evening. The passengers were mostly officers and soldiers; they were very agreeable companions, and we were conversing gaily when suddenly the train stopped. All looked out to discover the reason, but drew back their heads again in dismay, for on all sides there was nothing to be seen but a moving mass of soldiers. We perceived that their intentions were hostile, that we were captured like mice in a trap, for, unconscious of danger, we were totally unarmed in the midst of an armed force.

They dragged us out of the cars. I endeavoured to obtain release on the plea of being an Englishman and totally unconnected with either party in the war, but they would listen to nothing; they pinioned me like the rest, and to all my arguments and entreaties answered gruffly—

"That's what you say, stranger, but I guess that as you're caught with a bad lot, you'll suffer with the bad lot; a fellow can only be judged by the company he keeps."

They kept us closely guarded in a small wooden building until the next morning, when at daybreak they took us out, pinioned as we were, and made us walk as fast as possible until we reached a neighbouring canal. There fifty of the number got into a large boat, which I recognised as the build of my friend Mr. Crighton.

They then fastened ropes round the waists of myself and companions, and attaching them to the barge compelled us to walk on the banks of the canal and thus drag them up the stream. This work is usually performed by a couple of mules, but no mules were to be had at such a time for love or money. The work was not very hard, but we were compelled to walk on until the evening, when they distributed a little food among us. After this they took possession of some carts belonging to neighbouring farmers, and put us into them with soldiers sufficient to guard us and prevent the possibility of escape, and drove us quickly into a thick and unfrequented part of the woody wilderness. We soon perceived that we were miles from any human habitation, but our captors never halted until a late hour at night, when we reached a square, low, wood building, which we soon found was to be our prison for the present at least.

It was surrounded by a strong, solid, and high iron fence, which precluded all hopes of escape; but even if we had succeeded in scaling it, we should have gained nothing, for we were miles from anything save camps of the enemy, and we should have been recaptured at once.

The soldiers took us out of the carts, and thrust us in silence into the dreary prison, giving to each a small allowance of food. The food was dry, although as good as we could expect under the circumstances, but we were sick at heart, and said we would rather die than eat it; and overcome by fatigue, threw ourselves down on some straw which was lying in the inner part of our prison, and endeavoured to sleep.

What the thoughts of my companions were

I know not, but my own were heartrending in the extreme. I thought of my wife, I thought of my child. What would become of them if I was kept in this dismal den for months, for years? And then I remembered the words of her last letter, the sacrifice she had offered for my conversion! I felt sure that it had been accepted, that she would never see me again, that I should die in that horrible prison. I remembered, too, my own prayer, how I had begged of God to give me temporal punishment for my many years of irreligion, and now this punishment was come, and I felt as if it was too terrible to bear; and I writhed in anger rather than in sorrow. I was about to give way to my feelings in that infidel language to which I had so long accustomed myself if thwarted in any way, when suddenly I was aroused by a gentle sound uttered in sleep by a young man who was lying close to me. His words were—"Lord, I accept this from Thy hands, Thy will be done!"

I looked at the pale, gentle countenance of the youth by my side, and I perceived that he was a young ecclesiastic. His words turned the current of my ideas, and instead of giving way to anger and despair, I repeated his words.

I tried to repeat them from my heart, and they brought peace to my soul.

After a time we all arose and went out into our little yard, as the pangs of hunger were beginning to be felt, but the small heap of food, which was still lying in the corner, looked so untempting that none of us could make up our minds to taste it, excepting the young ecclesiastic: he approached, took a crust of bread, ate it, and then drank a little water out of the pitcher. He afterwards told me what an effort it was to do this; but he had long been accustomed to mortification, as he had lived for some years in a monastery, and therefore took the food simply to support nature. After a time hunger compelled us all to do the same, and the only event which broke the monotony of our existence was when our captors brought us this food once in twenty-four hours.

On the first days of our incarceration we walked up and down our dismal abode and talked a little, each endeavouring to pass the time and amuse the rest by tales of the past,— anecdotes giving their ideas of future chances, and so forth; but as time went on and no change came to break the monotony of our lives, we most of us became cross and irritable and surly; if one attempted to speak the other contradicted and silenced him. The only person who did not seem to lose patience was the young ecclesiastic. He looked ill, he looked depressed, but no one ever heard him utter a word of complaint or unkindness. I felt drawn towards this good young man; the example of his patience tuoched me—I felt moved to imitate his virtuous conduct. I sat down by his side one day and tried to converse in a low tone, so as not to be heard by the others; I asked him to tell me something concerning his former life.

He had not much to recount. He was the son of good and pious parents who had taught him to serve God from his infancy. He had been ordained priest only a few years before, and came over to America with the intention of becoming a missionary among the Indians. He had been spending a few weeks with a friend before going to the missionary college; when on his way back to Baltimore he was taken prisoner in the train like myself.

I thanked him for this little narrative, and I told him all about myself—my secret marriage and my sudden conversion from infidelity.

"But what I cannot comprehend," I exclaimed, when I had finished my relation, "is this: I begged God in the fervour of my repentance to send me some temporal punishment in expiation of my many years of sin and infidelity, and although the chatisement is more terrible than I could have thought possible, I feel I have no right to murmur or repine, and yet I do both murmur and repine at times; but *you!* you who have scarcely ever offended God wilfully, are involved in the same fearful misery as myself, but, far from complaining, there is always a look of peace, and almost happiness on your face. Tell me, oh! tell me, how you preserve this peace?"

The young priest looked at me compassionately and replied in a gentle tone—

"From my childhood I have been accustomed to see the will of God in every event, and in each trial a fresh means of purifying and saving my soul, *therefore* I cannot murmur at anything. But allow me, my dear sir, to observe that you take a wrong view of your troubles, you look upon them as direct judgments from Almighty God. Now I view them otherwise; they are not judgments, they are simply the natural course of events consequent on your own deeds. If you had acted as was your duty with regard to your marriage, if you had told your parents openly of it, and ran the risk of their displeasure, none of the sorrows that so often spring from secret transactions would have come upon you, they are the natural consequences of your fault. Again, if a person throws himself into danger by travelling unprotected in a country torn to pieces by civil war, he, of course, runs the risk of falling into trouble, even such trouble as that which has come upon us. Therefore, cease to look upon your sorrows as judgments hurled upon you by Almighty God, but look upon them as events which He has permitted to spring out of your own actions, but which events you may turn into gems of inestimable value, by bearing them with patience and accepting all in expiation of your many years of sin; instead of repining, rejoice! Be joyful, I say, for these days of apparent misery may be the steps which are to bring you to the enjoyment of that happiness of which St. Paul speaks, when he says, that "eye has not seen, or ears heard, the joys that are prepared for those who love God." Time seems long and dreary now, but still it is passing away. With regard to myself, I am quite certain that if our confinement is protracted many months that I shall not see the end of it, but be buried here, for my constitution is naturally weak; however, if it pleases God to allow this to be the case, I shall die content. My only grief will be the thought of never seeing my dear parents again in this world, but I shall leave them in the keeping of One who can watch over them far better than I can."

The words of this good young priest impressed me much, and I resolved to follow his advice and not murmur or repine, whatever might occur. But it was hard work, a dreary task,—nothing to do all day but pace up and down that miserable little abode. Our scanty summer clothing soon became insufficient to protect us from the weather, and our sufferings from the cold were great. At night we all huddled together on the straw in the sole place of shelter provided for us. Our captors brought us a few blankets and other articles of clothing, when the great cold set in, otherwise we must all have perished. Several among us had the noses and ears frostbitten. I narrowly escaped losing my nose, but I saved it fortunately by rubbing snow on it at once.

Months passed by, we were still in the same place, and our countenances and bodies became daily more pale and emaciated, but, by degrees, the weather grew milder, the days longer, and our sufferings consequently less severe, although we were become like animals, having almost lost the faculty of thinking and speaking. I seldom left the side of the good young priest, who became daily weaker and weaker, and could not rise even to fetch his coarse food, but I brought it to him, and fed him with the best bits I could select, as long as he was able to swallow anything, and never did he drop a word, or give the smallest gesture to denote impatience.

One evening, as I sat by his side holding his poor thin feverish hand in mine, he looked at me suddenly, and said in a scarcely audible voice—

"I am going fast, my last hour is come, may God bless you and reward you, my most kind

The Capture and Imprisonment. 371

friend, for all you have done for me. When God in His goodness admits me into Heaven, be sure that I will not forget you,—and will you promise that when you are set at liberty, and are once more in our dear native country, to go without delay to my bereaved parents and tell them all you can about me; and assure them, likewise, that I never forgot their religious instructions, and blessed and praised God to my last breath."

I pressed his hand, and promised everything, and I saw, indeed, even too plainly, that his life was ebbing fast, but he joined me in prayer to the last. He died so quietly that I scarce knew he was gone, until I felt his hand getting cold and knew that pulsation had ceased.

Then I closed his eyes, and crossed his hands over his breast, and I felt as if half my life was gone. I continued to sit by him as if stupefied. No one took any notice, no one cared, all were past thinking or grieving about anything.

And yet I felt as if he was near me, as if he was praying for me as he promised, for notwithstanding the greatness of our sufferings, I was calm—not the calm of stupidity, but the calm of resignation.

When our food was brought in the next

morning, the jailor as usual opened a small window, and looked into our sleeping room. He perceived that my young friend was dead, but went away without making a remark. He, however, soon returned, accompanied by a strong-looking heavily-built fellow carrying a pick-axe and a spade, who commenced digging, and between spade and pick-axe soon made a deep hole.

They then came and unlocked the door of our inner prison, entered, and immediately made me a sign to go out into the open part. I did not do so instantly, but on a second sign obeyed. All power of resistance was gone, and I staggered out to the exterior, from whence I could see what went on within.

They took the corpse of my young friend, and carried it out of the prison, and then placed it in the hole they had dug, and soon covered it over with the earth and the clay that the countryman had thrown out. They thought no more of it than if they had buried a dog or some wild animal. I scarcely know how time passed after this, it might be days, it might be months, the same dreary, weary monotony.

Another of our party died; he was found

dead in a corner on the straw; he was buried like my poor friend,—no one grieved, no one missed him, there was a little more food for each, and an extra blanket, but we cared neither for the one or other.

CHAPTER XXIII.

THE RELEASE.

ONE morning our jailor came at an earlier hour than usual, opened our door, and desired us to follow him. We did so, almost mechanically, not knowing what was going to happen; and, in truth, scarcely caring.

From long confinement and scanty food we were become so weak as scarcely to be able to walk, which our jailor perceiving, brought some horses and carts, made us get in, and drove us towards a railway dépot. He then told us to alight, and informed us that we were at liberty to go where we pleased, as peace had been proclaimed between the North and South, that all prisoners were released, and might rejoin their friends as soon as they pleased.

We listened in silence, being too weak and too much broken down in mind and body to feel anything like joy. Indeed, I almost believe we should then have preferred being left quiet in our dreary prison.

But there was no choice. We each received a loaf of bread, and a very small sum of money, and were left to wander where we pleased. No cruelty was intended, but it was impossible to make adequate provision for the numerous prisoners who were released on that day.

My companions and myself separated in silence. I went to the dépot and asked a porter if I could be taken to Baltimore. He looked at me distrustfully, and asked whether I had money to pay the fare. I replied that I had only one half dollar in the world, for that I had been imprisoned for many months, but that I had friends in Baltimore who would pay when I reached that city (I thought of the good archbishop). The official shook his head and replied—

"If we took folks on trust, our cars would be filled in no time at all, and if your friends failed I should be answerable for the debt, and I am a poor man. I would help you if I could, but in this I cannot. Have you no friend nearer to whom you could telegraph? I instantly thought of my good friend near Cumberland, Mr. Crighton. Directly I mentioned his name the porter brightened up and said—

"Is that gentleman your friend? If so, all is right; I have known him for years. He is immensely thought of in these parts, and respected by all, both North and South. He has much property in Maryland, and gives employment to thousands. If you write him a line I will take your letter with me by this train and deliver it to him."

He gave me a pen and ink and a bit of paper, and I wrote in a hand resembling that of a half-paralysed old man these few words—

"My good Friend,—I have been in prison all these months, I am penniless and ill, come to my assistance, I beg of you."

Almost before I could hope that my note had reached its destination, a telegram arrived from my friend to the head official of the dépôt, saying—

"Let the gentleman come on at once to Cumberland. I am answerable for all.

"H. Crighton."

And so I got into the train, and remained

until we reached Cumberland. No sooner did the train stop, than I saw my friend on the platform looking out. He entered the car, walked through, but did not recognise me until I spoke. And no wonder, for eleven months' misery had changed me completely. I was pale, wan, dirty, dishevelled, and my clothes were a mere set of dirty rags.

Tears of compassion filled the eyes of my friend for a moment when he looked at the wreck before him, but he shook my hand warmly and said in an encouraging tone—

"Cheer up, my friend, we will soon make you all right again."

When the porter delivered my note he described my miserable condition, therefore Mr. Crighton had brought a large cloak with him, which completely covered me, and he then led me to his carriage, where I was soon comfortably seated, and we started immediately for his residence, which we reached in a few hours; and I recognised, with inexpressible gratitude, that I was indeed in the hands of a "good Samaritan," for his amiable lady was at the door to greet us, and I was quickly taken to the comfortable apartment she had prepared, where I found a warm bath, a complete change of linen and other garments selected from the wardrobe of her husband, and a clean soft bed all ready for me to enter, as soon as I came out of the bath. I was reduced to such a complete state of weakness, as to be almost helpless, but Mr. Crighton and his factotum, Michael, assisted me,—my miserable remnants of clothing were soon carried out of the room and burned. Mrs. Crighton cut my hair herself, and Michael shaved me, and after that, my friend and his factotum assisted me to get into the nice soft clean bed, and I felt as no man can feel but one who has undergone the misery I had endured for eleven months. Mrs. Crighton soon after came to the door with a cup of excellent warm soup, which revived me still more, and they then all left me to try and get a little sleep.

My strength was so exhausted that it was many days before I was allowed to leave my room, but the fine clear air of the mountains, joined to the constant care and excellent nursing of Mr. and Mrs. Crighton, soon restored me in appearance to something like what I was before my imprisonment.

The first time I was allowed to go out in the carriage I begged my kind hostess to take me to the parish church in the valley below, that I might there thank God for my deliverance, and beg a blessing on my future life.

I wrote to my parents, and to my wife, as soon as possible, to let them know I was alive, and I will read you the letter to my father, as I have a copy which I chanced to keep, and I can read its contents more easily than I could recount them.

The stranger then took out his pocket-book, and having opened it, drew forth the letter in question, and commenced reading it to the interested group around him:—

"BELOVED FATHER AND MOTHER,—You have for many months, I doubt not, wept for me as for one whom you would never see again in this world, for my long silence must have made you conclude that by some fatal chance I had lost my life, and although (I confess) you have had much to complain of in my conduct in your regard, yet I know you loved me, and faulty as I have been, I loved you tenderly—indeed, I did.

" I was about to return to England, and was

on my way to Baltimore, when, in passing through a tract of country in which the war was raging fearfully, the train in which I was travelling was suddenly stopped, and we found ourselves surrounded by a hostile force. It was in vain for me to plead being an Englishman, and unconnected with the war, I shared the fate of my companions, and we were kept in close captivity for eleven months. Two of our number died, and I had so completely made up my mind that I could not survive much longer, that I now feel as if a new life had been granted me, and that the first act of that new life must be to repair my one great fault in your regard, my own dear parents, by revealing the long-concealed fact, that I am married. I have been secretly married for more than eight years, and I am married to the daughter of that man who you swore should never be allied to your family. I kept my marriage concealed lest you should carry out the threat you had once uttered in my presence of leaving any child of yours, who married without your consent, penniless. I know full well that you had the power of doing this, for your confidential servant, old Bramble (who hated that family as much as you did), often told me that you had full and entire control over your property, and this he had learned from your lawyer, with whom he had much secret intercourse.

"But now, my dear parents, I grieve beyond expression for that pusillanimity, for that deceit which was so sinful in the sight of God. I conjure you to forgive me, I entreat you to receive my wife and my child into your arms; disinherit me, if you please, if your vow requires it, but forgive me, forgive my wife. You have not much to pardon her, it is true, for she abhorred this concealment, and constantly exhorted me to tell you the truth. Had I done so, how much suffering might have been saved, for it was want, want almost of the necessaries of life, which compelled me to go out to America at this dangerous time. I had invested the £1000, which my godmother left me, in coal and iron mines in Maryland, and not receiving a penny of interest I went out to try and discover the cause of my loss.

"I cannot imagine what my poor wife has done without money during all these months; she and my child must have been almost starving. I am writing to her, likewise, by this mail, to tell her that I am alive, but she may have left the cottage in the Highlands where we resided.

"I have another confession to make to you, likewise, beloved parents. It will give you some pain, but that pain will not be without some little alleviation. You know that when I left England I was a mere sceptic, with no religious belief at all. By chance, or rather I should say, by the providence of God, I made acquaintance when on board ship on my passage out with a pious and learned priest, whose words made me reflect deeply, and laid the foundation of my conversion, which was completed by an astounding and startling occurrence which I will relate to you some future time; now I will only say, that I was received into the Catholic Church by the Archbishop of Baltimore in the cathedral about ten days after my arrival, and I hope to serve God faithfully during the rest of my life. I will not ask forgiveness on this point, as I am very certain that both you and my dear mother will prefer my being a Catholic to a complete infidel.

"I am writing to my wife by this mail, but

The Release. 383

I feel very doubtful as to where she and my child may now be. She has grieved for me as dead during all these months, and she must have suffered the greatest pecuniary privations. Distress may have compelled her to apply to you, to implore assistance for herself and child, if such is the case tell me, oh! tell me, dear father, I beseech you, where she is. Let her know that I am alive, but if possible break the news to her by degrees; do not let her be told suddenly, for she is supposed to have disease of the heart, and any great joy, sorrow, or anxiety might cause sudden death.

"Do not be anxious about me now, beloved parents, for I am in the house, and receiving hospitality from one of the best, one of the most kind-hearted persons I have ever met with in this world, whose great thought seems to be how he can do good to all around him, and his wife is one with him in every noble and benevolent act. I shall remain with them until I am strong enough to undertake the voyage home, and when I reach England it is to you and to my mother that I shall first go, to implore, on my knees, forgiveness for past faults and a blessing on my future. When I have done this, and not before, I shall go to my sorrowing wife, to my beloved child, and bring them both as I hope to your arms and heart, and I trust we shall never more be separated for any length of time; my one thought will be that of rendering your remaining years and those of my dear mother happy."

I received an answer within the month from my father, but none from my wife, therefore I concluded she had, as I feared, changed her place of abode. The letter from my father was as follows:—

"MY VERY DEAR SON,—Could you have seen the excess of joy with which we once more beheld your handwriting, which we thought never again to see in this world, you would have felt how much we love you, and that every past fault is more than forgiven.

"In truth, I blame myself severely for so many things, that I may well be gentle and mild in your regard. I almost (as I may say) compelled you to concealment, by allowing you to believe that the revelation of your marriage would involve you in beggary. And yet, my dear son, if you had made up your mind to run all risks, and to speak openly and truthfully as you have done in your last letter, all the misery we have suffered would have been saved ; for I had not bound myself by oath to disinherit you if you married a member of the D—— family ; in fact, I had not the power to do so, as the estate was strictly entailed upon you by your grandfather, and that entail could not be broken without your consent. You misunderstood some words I said on the subject, and I would not undeceive you, as I fancied this belief would prevent your seeking a wife out of that family whom I detested from my heart.

"But if you had nobly braved my displeasure and revealed all, you would have been quickly forgiven ; our anger must have been soon appeased by the feeling that you trusted in our love.

"I will not, however, blame you too much, as I was fearfully in the wrong myself for thus deceiving you.

"With regard to your present religious belief, I can only say that I regard Catholics as one degree better than infidels, and this is as much as I can allow. Would to God that I could have had the happiness of seeing you return to that pure faith which your mother and I tried to the best of our power to instil into your young mind, but the wish is, I feel, vain; you are now of an age to judge for yourself, so I shall say no more on that subject.

"Now, to return to your secret marriage. I had long felt certain that there must be some reason, besides the love of hunting and fishing, to cause such long absences from home, and I had a strong inward conviction that your love was for a member of that execrable D—— family; but, far from endeavouring to penetrate the mystery, I used every means in my power to prevent the disagreeable fact from coming openly to my knowledge. I did not wish to banish you from among us, and yet I felt that I could not at once pardon you and receive your wife as my daughter. Therefore your mother and myself preferred that you should believe us ignorant and unsuspicious of anything connected with your secret.

"Years passed by, and when you informed us of your projected visit to America, we fancied you would confide the truth to us before sailing, but you did not, alas! for if you had found courage to do so, much pain might have been saved us all, even then.

"At first we heard from you regularly, therefore when your letters suddenly ceased, we were greatly alarmed, knowing the state of the country,—and our uneasiness became so intense that we actually wrote to her whom we knew to be your wife, to ask if she had received tidings of you.

"She replied that your letters to her had likewise totally ceased, and that she was in the most terrible state of anxious fear, for she was certain you would not have neglected writing unless ill, or confined in prison somewhere.

"Our sorrow on receiving this communication was great, but we felt nothing but anger in regard to her whom we looked upon as the sole cause of our bereavement; and I grieve to say that I wrote an angry and stern letter to your wife, which has filled me with remorse ever since, although I then thought the provocation justified it. I reproached her, in unmeasured terms, for drawing you into a secret marriage without our consent. I told her that this underhand transaction had called down the curse of God, that we were deprived of our only child, and she of her husband, but that she should remain a beggar, as I would never give her a shilling, and that I would take our grandchild from her as she had no means of supporting it. I assured her that the law would allow me to take it by force, if necessary, in order to bring it up in its proper position, as she was a mere pauper.

"I wrote this letter in anger and wrath. I looked upon your wife as the cause of our sorrow, and I wished to make her feel it, but before a month was over I had repented my harshness, and regretted what I had written to her, to which I received no answer.

"My next epistle was much milder, and I said that my wife and myself had resolved to forgive her for the sake of our lost son, and that we would receive both herself and child into our home, and give them every comfort in our power. This was, however, returned to me by your old servant, who added a few lines to inform me that she was totally ignorant as to where her poor mistress and the child were gone. She said that my first letter had filled her with such excessive terror that she determined to leave at once, lest the child should be taken, but was quite undecided as to whether she would go to her old maiden aunt in Wales, and implore her protection, or whether she would go over to America, in the vain, undefined hope of hearing something of her husband if he was ill there.

"She had packed up her few effects quickly, and started the following night hurriedly, promising that she would write, either from her aunt's house in Wales, or from New York, as soon as she was settled down anywhere. But the servant had never received a line, and having promised not to write and make inquiries from any one, lest the secret should be betrayed, she had had no communication with the aunt, but sent me her direction that I might do so if I pleased. She, however, added that her fear was that both mother and child had sailed in an emigrant ship which left Liverpool about that time and was lost. She had procured a list of the passengers, and as a young woman with a young child was mentioned, she thought it more than probable that it was them, for the name told nothing, as Agnes intended to take her ticket under an assumed name.

"I wrote immediately to the aunt, and the answer I received was short and unsatisfactory—

"'SIR,—It is upwards of twelve years since I have seen niece Agnes. She never loved me, neither did I love her, for she pushed my white cat into a tub of water. If she had come to me at the time you mention I should have refused her admittance.

"'Excuse more, for I am in a state of the greatest anxiety at the present moment; my favourite black cat was caught in a trap this morning, and I much fear its leg is broken.

Yours faithfully.'

"Notwithstanding the total want of feeling displayed by these words, I have since written many times to the aunt, in hopes that your wife and child might have turned up later. Her answer was usually a curt 'No,' and 'I hope she never will.' I therefore fear that they must have perished in that emigrant ship."

The commencement of my father's letter had given me pleasure and comfort, but oh! how shall I express the grief with which my heart was filled when I read the rest. I gave a suppressed groan, the paper fell out of my hand, and I sat as one petrified, with despair depicted on every feature, and without power to move.

My sympathising host and hostess were by my side in a moment, but they knew not what to say ; they were ignorant of the cause of my grief. I pointed to the last page of the letter, they read it, and understood all.

My hostess endeavoured to alleviate my grief by gentle words, and hopes for the best, while he endeavoured to persuade me to take a more hopeful view of the matter, so many of my fears were mere surmises which might have no foundation. My wife was, perhaps, all this time merely concealed somewhere with her child, and would re-appear as soon as it was publicly known that I was returned.

But their benevolent arguments brought no comfort to my mind. I felt certain that Agnes was dead, that I should never see her more, and I continued to stare vacantly and dejectedly at the letter. I felt as if my affliction was too great to bear, as if it perfectly overwhelmed me. I sat, I spoke not, I scarcely understood the words of my host and hostess, — they sounded like meaningless babble.

Suddenly I started up, remembering the prayer that had so often brought me comfort during my long imprisonment. I stammered forth—

"Lord, I accept this from Thy hands."

The words, although uttered almost mechanically, produced a magic effect upon my soul; they recalled to my mind in a moment the words of the young ecclesiastic—

"Do not regard these sorrows, bitter though they may be, as judgments from God. Look upon them as what they really are, the natural consequences of the faults and imprudences into which you have fallen, but consider them also as gems of inestimable worth, which, if accepted patiently, will form a bright crown for you in heaven."

My rebellious feelings were gone; I knelt in humble submission, but I felt that my remaining years in this world must be henceforth desolate and cheerless. I almost hoped that both mother and child had really met death together in the waves of the Atlantic, for I could not think of my child left alone without terror; I remembered how we had kept her in ignorance of her family name, and of everything connected with her lineage, lest her artless talk should any day betray our secret. If Agnes had died suddenly, what had become of my Lily? Then, again, I pictured them to myself as shipwrecked on their passage to America, and bad as this might be, yet even that was better than for my loved one to be left alone without a friend to cherish or take care of her. I shuddered, I could not help it, but at the same time with these heartrending thoughts there was a constant mingling of the words—" Lord, I accept this, even *this*, from Thy hands."

My bodily weakness was so excessive, that the doctor whom Mr. Crighton called in would not allow me to think of returning to England for some weeks. I submitted, without a murmur, to remain as long as my kind host wished. What had I, indeed, now to make me sigh for home? Agnes was gone, my child was not found; the bright star of my existence was set, set to rise no more, I was alone! Oh! what does that word *alone* express,—misery, yes, misery.

At last I felt fit to undertake the voyage to England, and I bade farewell to my kind host and hostess. Mr. Crighton would not let me leave his residence alone, but accompanied me to New

York, as it was thought better for me to take the shorter passage from New York to Liverpool, and he saw me comfortably established in one of the best berths on board the large steamer. He did not leave until he had recommended me particularly to the care of the captain, and arranged everything he could imagine for my well-being during the voyage.

He then bade me farewell with the warmest expressions of regard and good wishes for my future; I on my part could scarcely utter the word farewell, so much did I feel the sympathetic benevolence that had been shown to me by both; but he maintained his hopeful cheerfulness to the last, and said, as he shook my hand—

"Keep up your spirits, my good friend, it is a long lane that has no turning; you have had your share of sorrow, bright days will return after a bit, depend upon it."

I got well through my voyage, the ship reached Liverpool in nine days. I merely remained there one night to recruit, and then started for my father's home in Scotland.

My reception from both parents was most tender. We were all deeply affected, and they

The Release.

found me so changed by all I had undergone, that they could scarcely recognise me. Almost my first question was—

"Have you any tidings of Agnes, or my child?"

No answer was returned, and the sad expression of their countenances told me the truth.

I could not settle down until I had visited the house where I left Agnes and my child, but I gained nothing by my journey there, save the certainty that she had left, and that no paper or document of any kind was to be found to enlighten the dark mystery.

I returned to my parents, and remained with them until it pleased God to call them out of this life within a year of one another. I then came into possession of a large income, which seemed almost a burden to one who had lost all that he loved, but I endeavoured to spend it in such a manner as I knew to be pleasing in the sight of God.

I have now been shown, by the dying request of my child, that there is a particular act of charity designated for me to perform, and I shall at once commence all that is necessary to ensure its success. When that is accomplished, God will doubtless point out to me by circumstances what He next requires, and will give me the power to carry it out, whatever it may be, for I desire nothing now in this world but to prepare for that happy abode where sorrow and care will be no more.

I have made every inquiry from poor old Biddy as to what my child told her concerning the death of her mother, which was caused, as I feared, by that heart disease which the doctors had always predicted would terminate her life if she had any great fright or anxiety. I likewise know from the good old woman the many trials and sufferings undergone by my dearest child, left thus alone and unprotected.

Yes, all this sorrow, this misery, was caused by deception. I tremble when I think of my first step in that dread path! But it is too late, let others take warning by my example.

The dying request of my loved one shall be, as I said, carried out exactly according to her desire, and I shall thus save many poor orphans from the misery I brought to my own pure and innocent child.

The stranger then arose from his seat, and having thanked his friends warmly for their heartfelt sympathy, said he must now say farewell, as business of importance required his presence in Scotland, and he must leave by the first train the next morning, but that they should hear from him occasionally, as he could not lose sight of those who had felt so much compassion for him, and that he should hope to receive good counsel from his host regarding the new institution, as he knew him to be an excellent man of business.

All were pleased with this proposal, the stranger departed at the time he named, and kept his promise of writing quickly.

Years passed by, the institution was completed, and the stranger found that peace and happiness in his latter years, which he had sought in vain before his voyage to America.

www.ingramcontent.com/pod-product-compliance
Lightning Source LLC
Chambersburg PA
CBHW050851300426
44111CB00010B/1221